MW00464145

GOD BLESSED TEXAS
& ME TOO

BRADY SEALS

ISBN-13 PAPERBACK: 978-1-7359526-0-4
ISBN-13 EBOOK: 978-1-7359526-1-1

EDITOR: ANDREW VAUGHAN
GRAPHIC DESIGN BY: CANDY THOMAS VAUGHAN
PRINTED IN THE UNITED STATES OF AMERICA 2020

TABLE OF CONTENTS

DEDICATION

Evan,

I wrote this book for you. I wanted my words to always be with you. They're meant to comfort and guide you. When you feel alone, pull this book out and dust it off. Read my words and hear my voice inside your head. You're not alone. Learn from my mistakes and choose a Godly path for your life. Know that God is always with you too. I promise He will not ever lead you astray. I love you bud. -Dad

Evan Seals and Brady Seals
Photo Credit: Rising Smoke Photography

PREFACE

This memoir has been in the making for a very long time. A couple of years ago I found a page or two of my writings on my old Mac laptop that dated back to 1993. I've written on and off through the years but never really got serious about it until my separation with my ex-wife in 2017.

That year was extra hard for me. I signed my divorce papers the following year and I got closer to God than I had ever gotten before. I read every self help guide I could, I saw three Christian therapists, I went to church every Sunday, I stayed up late watching pastors on YouTube, I held Bible studies, I prayed and fasted and felt the Holy Spirit encouraging me to write.

I don't want to be presumptuous, but I thought maybe my story could possibly help someone out there in their struggle. My despair was divorce but everyone goes through their own hard times. It may be a family member losing their fight to cancer, bankruptcy or some other life altering event.

I pray that you; the reader will see how God was beside me through all of my trials and tribulations. And how He has also blessed me abundantly in so many ways. To Him be the glory!

I don't believe in any way that it was God's Will for my ex-wife and I to get divorced but I do believe He took that hardship and used it for good. After she left, I was in ruins but He made me believe I could rebuild. His Word, influential teachings and appointed people, convinced me that I could be a stronger person, a more resilient Christian and a better father to my son, Evan.

If nothing ever comes of this book other than Evan learning about God's grace and mercy in my life, then mission accomplished. I want him to know that The Lord has been at the helm of my ship the entire time.

The book starts at the height of my success when I was still in the country band Little Texas. It talks about how we split up and how I managed to recover from it. I go on to tell about my solo career and also fronting the band, Hot Apple Pie.

You as the reader will go through the grief I experienced when I lost my Mom and Dad and other significant loved ones. Hopefully you'll observe the power of God's healing hands at work and see that He was the one that got me though. And maybe, just maybe, I'll also cause a few snickers and grins when you read about a few of my ridiculous road stories.

The stories, the people, the conversations and the places of this book are as I remembered them. Some details have been intentionally left out due to their sinful nature.

I also wish I could say that everything in the memoir is one hundred percent accurate, but I can't. My memory has faded over the years. However, I tried with diligence to research the timeline and even asked others about their recollection of how it all went down.

Please know this memoir is not meant to be scandalous or malicious. By no means would I ever intentionally bad-mouth anyone. It's meant to help others and shine a spotlight on The King of Kings and Lord of Lords. I want everyone to know who appears in this book that I love them.

I also want to put in this disclaimer... I am not a preacher. I don't have formal training in Hebrew or Greek and I'm not a theologian. The scriptures in the Bible are often misused and misinterpreted, so I apologize if my understanding is flawed. Again, I've tried to take the necessary steps to research the verses the best way I could.

I highly recommend taking the time to dive into God's Word on your own. Don't just take my word for it. Find out God's truth for yourself. Studying the Bible has been so rewarding for me through the years and it's helped me in so many ways that I can't describe.

It's funny...I can read a scripture one day and it means one thing and then years later I'll read the same scripture and it means something completely different. I think it's called "The Living Word" for a reason. *"For the Word of God is alive and active. Sharper than any double-edged sword, it penetrates even to dividing soul and spirit, joints and marrow; it judges the thoughts and attitudes of the heart."* *-Hebrews 4:12 NIV*

I want to thank everyone that contributed to this memoir and I want to especially thank Andrew Vaughan for his editorial skills. He's been very instrumental in helping me structure the book so it's easy to read.

For those interested, I plan on releasing new music that will coincide with some of the stories in the book and I plan to re-record some of my past hits, so be on the lookout. I also have plans to release another book in the future about my early years. I want to go back in time and show how God made the dreams of a little boy that lived on Hardell Drive in Fairfield, Ohio come true.

I couldn't have written this book without the stories in it. Which means I couldn't have done it without the people that's graced my life. So, thank you all! And to everyone that's been kind enough to purchase this book and read it, I appreciate you so very much. Enjoy!

ACKNOWLEDGEMENTS

In an attempt to not leave anyone out, I have listed as many people as I can who have played a key role in my life.

God
My Mom & Dad
Evan James Seals
Deni Baker
All of my family
All of my pets
My counselors
My childhood friends
My school friends
My teachers
My preachers
My musician friends
Everyone at the record labels
Everyone that had anything to do with my music career
Everyone at the management companies
Everyone at the booking agencies
Everyone at the publishing companies
All the video production crews
All of the venues I've performed
All of my fans
Every radio station that's played my songs
All my legal advisors

Acknowledgements

Volunteers at Music City Pickers LIVE!
Sponsors
My road crews
My co-writers
Greg Robinson
Debi Seals Mitchell
TJ Seals
Troy and Jo Ann Seals
Angie and Jeff Kenworthy
Kristie and Dave Young
David and Mary Jacobs
Mike, Brenda & Carrie Hubka
Spencer "Spanky" Bassett
Gordon Kennedy
Ricky Skaggs
Vola Ballew
The Hill Bunch
Jared Messer
Little Texas
Brad Pickel
Josh Logan
Ronnie "Saucerhead" Sawyers
Mike Shipley
Greg McDowell
Greg Caudill
Sandy Powell
Jim Prater
Larry "Coma" Blevins
Buck Blevins
Andy Sturmer
Hot Apple Pie
Steve Cochran
Tweedy

Acknowledgements

Stretch
Rusty Davis
MusiCares
Tommy Townsend
Richard Landis
Tracy Brown
James Stroud
Scott Borchetta
Joe & Linda Chambers
Blanche Carter Gronemeyer
John Carter Jr.
Kenneth Bates
Brian and Nancy Eckert
Greg Strizek
Dave Fowler
Bill Whyte
Rhonda Funk
Dumpy Rice
Brian Rice
Paul Jefferson
Stan Lynch
Richard Marx
Kevin Schuck
Tyler Amp Works
Jane Walker
Gabe Hernandez
Alan Dysert
The McDowell Family
Cassandra Tormes
Don Reilly
Lisa Stewart
Gateway Franklin Church
Steve Emily

Acknowledgements

Ty Smith
Lua Crofts Faragher
Jimmy Seals & Dash Crofts
Brian Russell
My Facebook Friends
Tiffany Jones
Roxane Barlow
Devon O'Day
Nicole Zeller
Brickshore Media
Amy Willis
Trisha Walker
Richard Courtney
Glyn Patterson
Regie Hamm
Callie Day
Durward Blanks
Tiffany Berry Henwood
Kristin Fisher Anderson
Mark Nesler
Colby Balch
The Heimerdinger Foundation
Kathie Heimerdinger
Katharine Ray
Judy Medford
Lynda Davenport
Dr. Propper
Harpeth Hills Church of Christ (Salt Class)
Rodney & Claudia Crowell
Burt and Sanna Stein
Andrew Vaughan
Candy Thomas Vaughan
Christy DiNapoli

Doug Grau
Hamstein Music
RPM Entertainment
Scott Siman
Bill Mayne
Alison Prestwood
Danny Flowers
Tommy Barnes
Jeff Glixman
Phil Ehart
Jim Gentile
Lily Salinas
Aaron Benward
Brian McComas
Steve Navyac
Jackie Williams
John and Kim Scott
Clif & Debbie Doyle
Ron Baird
Dan Grimes
CAA
Buddy Lee Attractions
Lou & Sheree Spoltore
Live Arts & Attractions
Rod Essig
Gene Dries
Gerry Wenner and his film crew
The Sunset House
Stephen Allen Davis
The Petty Junkies
Mike "Juice" Kyle
Phil Bennett
Dawn Nepp

Acknowledgements

Gary Haber
Buddy Hyatt
Jay Hall
Suntrust Bank
TriStar Bank
On-Stage Stands
David Vincent
Takamine
Mario Martin
The Factory at Franklin
Allen & Bright, PC
Monica Maciel
Talent Concepts
Helen "Sissy" Treat
615 Entertainment
Jim Ed Norman
Bob Saporiti
Warner Bros. Records
DreamWorks Records
StarCity Recording
Image Entertainment
Steven "Herky" Williams
Willie Nelson
ClearBox Rights
Soundcheck
NSAI
ASCAP
Nashville Musicians Association, AFM Local 257
SAG-AFTRA

CHAPTER ONE:
LONG-HAIRED COUNTRY BOYS

"And when he was at the place, he said unto them, Pray that ye enter not into temptation." -Luke 22:40 KJV

1991 was the year everything went into hyperdrive for Little Texas. We released our first single to radio off our debut album *First Time For Everything* called "Some Guys Have All The Love". We'd come a long way in a short amount of time. From paying our dues on the road and being finalists on the televised talent show "Star Search" to getting a record deal at Warner Bros. and making our very first music video. The band had ditched our cramped van for a spacious tour bus, and progressed from playing smoke filled honky-tonks to performing in fifteen thousand seat arenas.

Life had changed dramatically for me. My childhood seemed so distant, even though I was still only twenty-one. God had answered my prayer of wanting to become a successful musician. It all happened lightning fast. When I went out on the road for the first time at sixteen, I thought it would take at least ten years before I got my shot at the big leagues. God did it in half the time. I was blessed, for sure.

The speed of the blessing had an unexpected effect on me though. I went from the shelter of a Pentecostal Sunday school in Fairfield, Ohio to the excessive enticements of the world. I had been a Christian for as long as I could remember and was baptized around the age of nine. So, I knew God. I was saved, but I was getting sidetracked.

I wasn't anywhere near as close to God as I used to be. With the hustle of this new life, I got into the habit of ignoring God's warning signs of danger. I was naive and exposed to the devil's dealings. I was living it up. I'm sure my mom and dad worried about me every day and no doubt they were praying overtime that I wouldn't lose my way.

Vanity had also become an issue. My appearance on stage had become a big deal since I was in the public eye all the time. I felt I needed to portray a certain kind of image. I had always been an Elvis fan when I was a kid and I thought his black leather motorcycle suit that he wore in his infamous '68 Comeback Special was the coolest.

I felt like I wanted to have that same kind of "rough boy" image. Even though I never gave my parents any trouble growing up, I felt a little rebellious inside. And now that I was out on my own and living the rock and roll lifestyle, I thought it'd be alright to embrace it.

Everybody in the band had grown their hair out and each of us had our own signature style. The '80s rock and roll style was still alive and well. Del's thing was black spandex shorts and a button-down shirt with cowboy boots. Propes usually had torn up jeans and was known for playing his black Steinberger headless bass. Porter always wore a vest. Tim sported a fringe jacket and Dwayne O'Brien wore black sleeveless shirts. I went back and forth between motorcycle jackets and big pirate looking shirts. I have no clue as to why I felt like pirate shirts were cool, but I did.

Little Texas at The Grand Ole Opry
From left to right: Porter Howell, Brady Seals, Tim Rushlow

As I was preparing this book, I contacted Little Texas' old manager, Christy DiNapoli. I wanted to know what he remembered about the release of our first song, "Some Guys Have All The Love". This was his response...

I believe we were in Denver when Porter played it for me. We carried a small tape recorder with us and you and O'Brien went into your room, set up the Yamaha keyboard on the AC unit and you laid down a version with the signature lick and keyboard part all the way through with O'Brien singing. We then ended up in Dallas/Fort Worth at the Crystal Chandelier for a week. We worked up the new songs during the day, but this one just didn't feel good. I told Del to change the drum pattern to more of a Phil Collins syncopated 16th note high-hat snare thing to make the song move and create a fun up-tempo feel along with your signature keyboard lick. That's when the song came alive!

We recorded it over the sound system at the club, I played it for Doug (A&R at Warner Bros. Records) when we got back to Nashville and it made the first session with us and James (Stroud). We recorded it over at Treasure Isle (recording studio in Nashville) along with four others, it was the last one on the CD that we gave to the label. They distributed it to the staff and everyone picked this one as the first single. I thought the mix was really flat, so we brought in Chuck Ainlay to remix it over at Masterphonics and he took it to another level sonically. We got a single release date then shot a $20,000 video and shipped the single to radio and the video to CMT.

Before we went for adds, we flew a bunch of radio programmers and consultants to Dallas for a show at Cowboys, a golf tournament the next day and then took them to meet Nolan Ryan and watch a Rangers game. The following Monday we had 32 stations add the record out of the box and it went all the way to #6.

Little Texas meeting Nolan Ryan

My experience at the Texas Rangers game was unforgettable. Little Texas not only invited radio programmers to the game like Christy said, but we also sang the national anthem that day. After we sang, we were able to shake hands with the legendary pitcher, Nolan Ryan. That was huge for me having been a pitcher myself. He was a childhood hero. Every time we played backyard baseball; I was Nolan. His fastball was insanely fast which in my mind, made mine faster.

The game day would only get more bizarre as the hours rolled past. After leaving the mound on the baseball diamond we all made our way back to our seats to watch the game. I sat down next to none other than George W. Bush. We shook hands and exchanged some small talk. He told me he was one of the owners of the

Texas Rangers and we settled in to watch the game. We sat there through all the innings and rooted for the home team and ordered hot dogs. He was as cool as they come. By the time the game was done we had enjoyed several in-depth conversations about Texas and his baseball team. He definitely made an impression on me. I noticed how everyone around us gravitated to him. He was an extremely likable dude.

I was surprised to find out later that George W. was elected Governor of Texas in 1994. He used our song "God Blessed Texas" at his victory rally. I had no idea just how special those three hours at the Rangers game would be. Little did I know then that he would go on to become not only the Governor of Texas but the President of the United States!

Money started flowing in from all of the shows we were doing and I decided to make a down payment on my first house in Bellevue, TN. I didn't want to pay rent anymore and I needed a place to hang my clothes. A place to call home. I was still visiting mom and dad whenever I could but finding the time to get back to Fairfield was getting harder and harder to do. They would come down to visit or come see me if I was playing anywhere near Cincinnati.

I asked my old hometown friend, Greg McDowell if he'd like to be my roommate and look after the house when I was out on the road. The timing couldn't have been better because he had decided just months before that he wanted to move to Nashville as well.

He agreed and moved all his stuff in. I converted the upstairs bonus room into a recording studio and called it The Purple Room. I hung purple acoustic paneling on the walls and placed lava lamps in the corner to give it some atmosphere. I spent many nights writing and recording there.

Little Texas' follow-up release after "Some Guys Have All The Love" was the song "First Time For Everything" and suddenly it was 1992. The band continued to tour non-stop. We were all stoked when we found out that we were going to open for Clint Black at Caesars Palace in Las Vegas, Nevada. Clint was doing really well on the *Billboard* charts around that time. He was still riding the wave of his big hit singles like "Killing Time" and "A Better Man". After Vegas he asked us to do a string of dates with him on his, "The Hard Way Tour."

As a band we knew all about Clint's career because he was managed by Bill Ham who also managed and produced ZZ Top. Bill got involved in our career from a publishing standpoint. He also owned a music publishing company called Hamstein Music Group. Christy, our manager knew Dean Migchelbrink who was the director of business affairs there. All the guys in the band signed a publishing agreement around that time with Christy and Bill.

Clint was a class act. He and his crew treated us like kings. We instantly became friends with all of them. Rushlow was friends with Clint's keyboard and fiddle player, Jeff Huskins and we'd all hang out before and after the shows. At that time, I was really trying my best to get into shape and put on some weight. I was tired of being a string bean. Jeff was big into working out and showed me some of his secrets to gain muscle mass. He was a true-blue body builder. The dude was ripped!

Our monitor engineer at the time, Brad Pickel and I would hit the gym with him or anyone else that was willing to go every chance we could. We both bought bicycles to put under the bus so we could ride them to the nearest gym in every city we'd stop in. We were obsessed. We'd joke about our size and call each other "lizard" because we were so skinny.

Little Texas Days
Brady Seals

While out in Vegas with Clint we filmed our second video for "First Time For Everything" on the bridge of The Hoover Dam. I have no idea how we got cleared to film there but we did. All I remember is how hot it was and the view was incredible. We'd go on to release "You and Forever and Me", "I'd Rather Miss You" and "What Were You Thinkin'" off our album "First Time For Everything". All of the singles except for "What Were

You Thinkin'" were written by Porter and O'Brien. I was thrilled when we released "What Were You Thinkin'" in October of 1992 because it was my first radio release as a co-writer. Even though it only made it up to #17 on the charts, I was as proud as I could be.

Our booking agency, CAA (Creative Artists Agency) booked us on some overseas shows after our stint with Clint. Our original booking agency, Doyle Agency still sent us gigs from time to time but we had to go with a bigger agency simply because the demand for the band had increased. Fortunately, Clif and Debbie, the owners, completely understood our need to move on.

Flying to Europe for the first time was scary for me. Other than flying to Cuba with my first road band, Josh Logan and Sandy Powell, it was my first really long trip. I knew I had to suck it up and get over my fear of flying and try to get some sleep, and breathe slow and deep for the next nine hours.

We flew into London to play our first show at a small theatre with Mark O'Connor opening for us. Mark was considered to be one of the best violinists on the planet. I'll never forget that night being backstage and looking through a stage door that had a small round glass opening. All I could see was the silhouette of Mark, center stage with one big bright spotlight on him. He was alone. Just him and his instrument. He was making his violin sing. I thought to myself, "how are we going to follow that?"

I don't even remember the details of the show because my time schedule was all messed up because of jet lag. I guess we did alright. But I do remember that night we all got to meet the legendary British singer and producer Nick Lowe. He was probably there to see Mark, I'm just not sure. At the time I didn't realize just who I was shaking hands with. It was later in life before I understood just how significant and special that moment was. Nick and his band Rockpile became a big influence on me.

From London we traveled to Ireland, Switzerland and Germany. We played several shows with our label mate at the time, Jim Lauderdale. We all loved his music because it had a traditional thing about it that wasn't being played on the radio in the states at the time. The Europeans loved him though.

We also met up with The McCarters in Switzerland. They were a country music duo that had just come on the scene. They were two beautiful sisters and were as nice as they could be. We all hung out while we were there and took a day and climbed a towering mountain that was close to our hotel. We were all spellbound when we got to the top and saw one of the bluest lakes, we all had ever seen, nestled within the mountains. There were several canoes just sitting there for visitors to use for free, so we got in and paddled out to the middle to experience it. To this day it is the prettiest place I've ever visited.

Little Texas European Tour- Switzerland
From left to right: Brady Seals, Del Gray and Tim Rushlow

While in Germany we filmed a live performance for a television station. I've seen some of the footage of the show lately and it looks like the people in the crowd are scared and stunned. Ninety percent of the crowd were older people and I'm sure they were saying to themselves, "What in the world are we watching and listening to?" There we were with our hair half way down our backs looking like the heavy metal band, Motley Crüe, rockin' out but playing country music. I know they were bewildered.

Once we got back into the states it was full steam ahead. We were everywhere. We'd visit radio stations during the day and play shows at night. Every spare moment we were promoting our newest single. While we had down time in our hotel rooms, we were all assigned certain radio stations to call and thank them for adding our single. Management also had us performing on every TV show that would have us.

I remember the first time we performed on TNN's (The Nashville Network), Nashville Now with Ralph Emery. I had lost my voice. Looking back on it now, I'm not sure if I was sick or I was just really nervous to be on television. All I know is, I couldn't sing. Thankfully, my part was the least missed. I usually sang the really high part that doubled the low harmony. I just acted like I was singing and got through the performance.

Two years later that experience would come in handy when a new artist named Faith Hill would open for us. She was also signed to Warner Bros. and she had the opportunity to debut her new single that night, "Piece of My Heart" along with the other songs on her new album. She had lost her voice too and was nervous and embarrassed. I told her about my experience on TNN and explained to her that it just happens sometimes and everything will be ok.

Hopefully, it made her feel like she wasn't alone. It turned out her voice issue was not just being nervous but she had a ruptured blood vessel on her vocal cords. She went on to have surgery to repair the damage. When she returned, she really returned. Boy, did she ever make her mark on country music. She's now regarded as one of the best female vocalists to ever come out of Nashville.

While we were touring, we were writing and even recording. We knew that we had to follow our first album with something big. I was writing down song titles all the time. I'd get in my bunk at night and listen to music and would hear song titles in the lyrics I was listening to. It didn't seem like there were enough hours in the day to get it all done. The pressure was on to come up with hit songs.

I was one of the primary songwriters at this point. O'Brien and Porter had been doing most of the writing but I kicked into high gear. I even talked to our manager and publisher Christy to have him hook me up with some writers, outside the band, to see if something magical would happen. He went to Dean at Hamstein Music and Dean suggested that I write with Jerry Lynn Williams.

The next thing I knew I was on a plane to Tulsa, Oklahoma, Jerry's hometown. I got off the plane with a limo waiting for me at baggage claim. I had been told that Jerry was "the real deal". He had written songs like, "Forever Man" and "Pretending" for Eric Clapton. He had contributed two songs, "Real Man" and "I Will Not Be Denied" to Bonnie Raitt's 1989 GRAMMY Award-winning album *Nick of Time*. He also wrote songs for B.B. King, Robert Plant and Stevie Ray Vaughan. This dude was a powerhouse!

I felt like a king riding in the back of that limo. I had prepared several song titles and a few melodies to play for Jerry and I was going over that in my head when the driver pulled up into a big ranch house and opened my door. I rang the doorbell and a pretty lady came to the door in her bathrobe. I was like, "Hi, my name is Brady" and she seemed preoccupied and said, "C'mon in hun, Jerry is back there in his music room...you can go on back." She directed me with a point of a finger where his music room was and I made my way back there.

When I got to the room, I noticed all of Jerry's gear was turned on but Jerry was nowhere around. I sat there patiently for what seemed like an hour. I didn't know what to do with myself so I just got up and made my way over to a keyboard and started playing a simple little melody. From another room I heard a voice yell, "Play that again!" I figured that was Jerry, so I did. I played it a few times when he finally emerged from the other room like a ghost. There were no formal greetings like, "Hey Brady, my name is Jerry...good to meet you" or "Hey man, how was your trip?" Nope, it was straight into the song. He started singing a melody over the chords I was playing and I just tried to keep up.

The melody I was playing sounded nothing like a Little Texas song. The lyrics he was singing were good, but very psychedelic. I remember thinking that there was no way this song would ever make the cut. We finished up the day with a mediocre song and I don't think I really ever got to know Jerry. He was a strange bird but I felt honored to be in the same room as him. I'm not really sure if Jerry ever turned the song into Hamstein or not. In fact, I don't know if my trip to Tulsa ever really happened.

I went on to have several incredible co-writes. One was with my uncle Troy Seals and Max D. Barnes. Both of them went on to become inductees into N.S.A.I.'s Songwriters Hall of Fame. It was the first time that I sat in a room with my uncle to write a song. I was so nervous and couldn't believe it was happening. I just sat there watching and listening to those two guys coming up with lyrics. They both were heroes of mine. These were the same guys that wrote George Jones' hit, "Who's Gonna Fill Their Shoes", Waylon's song, "Drinkin' and Dreamin'", Conway Twitty's honky-tonk standard, "Red Neckin' Love Makin' Night", Keith Whitley's, "Ten Feet Away" and Randy Travis' smash hit, "I Won't Need You Anymore (Forever and Always)".

Of course, I knew of Troy's success but I also knew exactly what Max had accomplished as well. It was like being in the room with Superman and Batman. They threw away lines that day that I would've died to keep. It made me realize just how far I needed to go to be a great writer. We wrote an old school country song that day but it wasn't quite in the vein of Little Texas, so it was never cut.

The other co-write that stood out was with Mentor Williams. He was the dude who wrote "Drift Away" for Dobie Gray back in 1972, the song would later be remade by Uncle Kracker. Many other artists like Allan Clarke, Roy Orbison, Humble Pie, Rod Stewart, Ike & Tina Turner, Waylon Jennings, Jon Bon Jovi, Ray Charles and Bruce Springsteen recorded it as well. Mentor was one of the sweetest souls I've met. We met out at Percy Priest Lake in Nashville and wrote under a big oak tree sitting at a picnic table. He was as humble as they come. We wrote a fine song that didn't make the cut, but man, it was incredible to write with him.

Opportunities were budding all around me like the leaves of that oak tree. It was one memorable moment after another. God was surely at work carving my path. It's easy to look back now and see what God was doing but it was a lot harder then.

I felt like the guy in The Eagles song, "Life In The Fast Lane". "*I was blowin' and burnin', blinded by thirst. I didn't see the stop sign and took a turn for the worst.*" I couldn't keep up with all the people I was meeting, the towns I was visiting and the doors that kept opening. I would be noticed nine times out of ten when I'd go into a restaurant or store. People started treating me differently which made me start treating them differently.

Whenever I would meet someone new, I would just wait for them to ask something from me like an autograph, free tickets to a show or backstage passes. It almost never failed that if I met a songwriter, they'd want to pitch me their songs for Little Texas to record. I couldn't blame them but I didn't feel like they were genuinely glad to meet me, I was just an income generator.

I also couldn't go home to Ohio without being bombarded with visitors over at Mom and Dad's house. I'd have to sneak in and out without telling anyone I was coming home. Suddenly I had friends and family that I never knew I had.

My dream had come true. The one that Mom and Dad and I had prayed for. I had asked and I had received. But it wasn't what I had imagined. Half the time I was happy and grateful, other times I was stressed beyond belief. I was traveling the world and sharing stages with my musical idols, but there was barely any alone time and very little family time. Time was not mine anymore. It belonged to the band and the crew, to our manager, to our producers, to the record executives and to the fans. There was too much money being made and too many deadlines. It felt like there were simply too many people relying on me and the band.

All my spare time had to be voted on by the committee. I couldn't do anything unless the band and management approved it. I was faced with the realization that playing music was now a job and I had committed to making it. There was no turning back and no way out. I had to write and perform, whether I wanted to or not. I felt cornered, and the pressure kept me up at night. It was beginning to make me physically sick. I knew I was lost. So I prayed, and I prayed. And I prayed.

THE CURIOUS WOLF

We've all seen it on those National Geographic shows. Where the pack of wolves are traveling in the winter snow going from one destination to another. The leader of the pack is out there in front, watching and guarding. He's the strongest one, the alpha male. We see the rest of the wolves trotting along behind him, trusting that the leader knows where he's going.

And then there's that one curious wolf, the wanderer, the instigator, the halfwit. He or she is the wolf that's easily distracted. The one that goes off by themselves, far from the security of the pack leader, to chase a rabbit into the woods. There they go, over one log, down a creek and through a thicket of pines before it hits them... they're lost.

That's how we can be when following God. I know that's how I was. I was too easily distracted. I was praying while out on the road but I wasn't learning and growing as a Christian. I didn't stay focused on Him. In my early '20s, I was slowly but surely getting further and further from God's Will. Over one log and down in a creek...I felt it deep down inside but I thought I could handle the temptation and sin. I didn't think I was straying too far. In reality I was backsliding. Growing up in a Pentecostal church, we used the term "backslider" all the time. It is a real term with a unique meaning in The Bible.

In Jeremiah 2:19 NKJV God says, *"Your own wickedness will correct you, and your backslidings will rebuke you. Know therefore and see that it is an evil and bitter thing that you have forsaken the Lord your God...."* Also, Jeremiah 3:22 NKJV says, *"Return, you backsliding children, and I will heal your backslidings."*

The story of Simon Peter comes to mind and how he denied Jesus. Peter had been a dedicated disciple of the Lord for three years and yet Peter denied Him in the end. He backslid.

I don't think we suddenly backslide. It's a series of missteps. Sin is a slippery slope. Each and every day, we are either strengthening or tearing down our spiritual character. We either move forward or fall backward.

Relying on self-knowledge, not praying and following God at a distance will send us backward every time. Stay near Him. We're going to fall back sometimes, there's no doubt. But we have to be aware of our failures and correct them quickly. We need to get back to the leader of the pack as fast as we can.

Chapter Two:
Big Time

"For the love of money is a root of all kinds of evil. Some people, eager for money, have wandered from the faith and pierced themselves with many griefs." -1st Timothy 6:10 NIV

Even at the height of Little Texas' success I was never a big partier. I would drink a beer or two every now and then, but that was about it. However, I did start smoking pot. I remember the first time I smelled it when I first went out on the road. I was green and sixteen. Literally! The aroma was earthy...like fresh pine trees. As far as cigarettes go, I have never ever tried them. As a kid, I didn't like the way they smelled. I inhaled second-hand smoke way too much over the years while playing all those dive bars to ever have the desire to give them a try. To this day I've never used any drug besides pot. I had plenty of chances to, but never had the urge. Looking back, I firmly believe that was the Holy Spirit protecting me.

When I would smoke marijuana, I thought it made me listen more intensely to music. That's probably not really true, but I thought it was true at the time. And plenty of musicians will tell you that pot heightens the musical senses. I'd put on headphones and I'd hear things I had never heard before. Bands like Pink Floyd, The Beatles and Queen suddenly sounded different. Some other bands I got into around that time were bands like Yes, Tom Petty & The Heartbreakers, ELO and Steely Dan. I had a new appreciation for the depth and substance in the recordings that I hadn't had before smoking.

Around that time, I fell in love with the California sound. Brian Wilson and The Beach Boys primarily. I couldn't believe that I had missed how special and influential their productions were. I also failed to notice just how extraordinary The Beatles were when I was young. I didn't realize how they changed pop music! All I remember was singing a medley of songs in choir class like "Hard Day's Night" and "Eight Days A Week" in high school. I couldn't appreciate how intricate and innovative their melodies and productions were.

I was growing up musically, and the direction of my songwriting started to turn. I wanted to go deeper. I wanted to write music that would influence others and make a difference to the listeners. I wanted to matter. I knew that it was time to try harder as a writer and musician. It was time to push myself to come up with lyrics and melodies that would make people want to put on headphones and dive deep into my songs.

Porter, Dwayne and I were writing incessantly. We all were pushing each other to turn in better material for the band. We knew the sequel to our first record needed to be more mature and substantial and we all thought the soft-rock sound and style of the Eagles, Jackson Browne and The Little River Band would be a good place to start.

One day after leaving Las Vegas on the back of the bus Porter, O'Brien and I were talking about our past loves. Each one of us had our own heartbreak story. Mine was Roxane Barlow, my first love. Each of us reminisced about our high school sweethearts and O'Brien started jotting down phrases and ideas. Porter started playing a chord progression that he and O'Brien had already been fooling with. We titled the song, "What Might Have Been". The three of us knew right then and there that it had something special about it. It became the song to beat for the second record.

The three of us got on a roll and wrote six out of the ten songs for the upcoming CD. Whenever we'd write something that had potential, we'd record it almost immediately. We were touring so much that we had a twenty-space rolling rack of recording gear that would be wheeled into the dressing room of every venue we played. So whenever we finished writing a song, we'd record it backstage.

Every year we'd take time off from touring to head to Nashville. All the country artists did. It was an event called Fan Fair. It's now called, CMA Fest. Back then thousands of country music fans would flood the Tennessee Fairgrounds to meet their favorite country artists. I think they paid around $80 a ticket for a week of concerts and special fan events where they could meet their idols. The Fairgrounds were very downhome. All of the horse stalls and big warehouses would be turned into artist booths. Each artist would rent the space to set up their own unique booth where they could meet their fans at set times. The event would happen in the summertime and it would get so hot in there you could fry an egg on the concrete floor.

Little Texas- Fan Fair
From left to right: Dwayne O'Brien, Porter Howell, Duane Propes,
Del Gray, Brady Seals and Tim Rushlow
Photo Credit: Christy DiNapoli

I remember the year where the band met at the main building where the artists check in. After putting "Artist" lanyards around our necks, they stuffed us in golf carts to take us to our booth. When we got to our building, we noticed a line that wrapped around the entire building. When we got closer, we found out that they were waiting to meet Garth Brooks. The guy was on fire at that time and there was nobody bigger on the radio. A couple years later he set a record for signing autographs for twenty-two hours straight!

Aside from taking country music to new commercial heights, Garth led the pack when it came to fan appreciation. The dude never let up. He would go out of his way to make sure each fan knew they were crucial to his success. He set the standard for all the country music artists at the time. We were all expected to do a meet and greet after the show whether we felt up to it or not. Personally, I thought that it took away some of the artist's mystery. Pop and rock artists would've never dreamed of giving so much access to the fans. Garth changed that.

Whenever I wasn't performing or promoting with Little Texas, I was home writing by myself or co-writing. One of my favorite co-writers was Tommy Barnes. He and I had become good friends and writing with him was effortless. One day over at his house, he played me "My Love". I knew the song was special after the first verse. It sounded like a hit to me. He had written most of the song by himself. I felt it needed tweaking though, if Little Texas was going to cut it.

The lyrics of his original chorus kept looping over and over, where it'd say, "My Love, are you ready for my love, my love? My love, my love is ready for you, my love" and then it would repeat. I asked him if he'd be cool if I played it for Porter and see if we could try and make it work for the band. Porter heard the potential in the song too and we immediately started fooling with the melody and lyrics of the chorus. It wasn't long before we made some changes and voila, the new version was born.

The melody of "My Love" is a beast to sing, typical for a Tommy Barnes song. It has a large vocal range that makes you think hard about where to take time to breath after each phrase. It was the last song to be recorded for the album and Tim sang it. Our producers, for whatever reason, wanted to hear me sing it. They had probably become used to hearing me sing it on the demo. I gave it a shot and it made the record. I had no idea then it would go on to become our third number one song off our CD, *Big Time*. A proud moment.

Chapter Two: Big Time

The van that Porter's dad had bought for us to tour in was long gone. We were now renting a bus and pulling a trailer with all of our gear in it. It was an expensive upgrade but we were doing way too many shows out west to keep driving those long distances. It was becoming brutal and flat out dangerous. There were many times where each one of us would come close to dozing off while driving.

When we first rented a bus, we hired my old bus driver friend, Coma, who drove the bus for my prior bosses, Josh Logan and Sandy Powell. Coma didn't turn out quite like Little Texas had hoped. He was getting up in his years and also smoked too many cigarettes, Pall Mall, I recall. Even if he'd crack a window while driving, none of us could stand the smell of them. We'd constantly feel the bus swerve and hit those grated sections of the interstate, warning drivers of the edge of the asphalt. It had become too dangerous to have him out there. The band hated to let him go but he understood and we parted ways amicably.

We then found a guy that lived outside of Nashville that owned a bus. I won't say his last name to protect his identity but I will give you the initial of his last name though. His name was James A. and James A. looked like Kenny Rogers with a toupee. It matched his salt and pepper beard. He'd spent a lot of time out in the sun because his face was sun splotched and leathery. If I'm not mistaken, he also had one or two silver capped teeth as well, but I could be making that up.

The guy had a good-looking bus that was probably from the late '70s or early '80s that he said he'd rent to us and he could drive it for us too. We all thought it was a pretty sweet deal, which we really needed at the time since money was still tight. It wasn't long before James A. told us he had a son named, James A. Jr. He told us that his son needed a job and would love to come out on the road and help sell merchandise for us. We all agreed to give James A. Jr. a try.

I knew after the first weekend run that James A. Jr. wasn't a good choice. I recall sitting in the back lounge with O'Brien and him telling me, Propes and Del about his conversation with James A. He said they were watching a Cowboys football game on TV in the hotel room when James A. Jr. started telling him a story about how he recently got arrested.

The conversation went something like this, "Yeah well I was over at this girl's house and we'd been messin' around you know. When all of a sudden, her boyfriend came in. I didn't know she had a boyfriend....I swear man. He busted in and had a gun and started shootin'. I rolled off the bed to get to my jeans 'cause I had my pistol in there and I needed to get to it." Then James A. Jr.'s attention went back to the TV. "Woo hoo, that was a great play right there."

"But anyway," he said. "I kinda felt a burnin' in my stomach, I didn't know until later I'd been shot. Well I got out my pistol and started shootin' back. I shot that mother..." And then just like that his attention was back to the game, "Touchdown!...Man that was a great run!"

O'Brien went on to tell about how James A. Jr. said he had been arrested and was now out on probation for first degree murder! My first thought was, how is this man able to cross the state line if he's on probation?

James A. Jr. didn't stay out with us too long and neither did his dad. We had several other crazy situations that happened in the weeks to come that made it clear that both of them had to go. We'd all realized that having them around was just trouble waiting to happen.

I recently asked our drummer, Del what else he remembered about James A. Jr. and his shenanigans. Del claimed that James A. Jr. told a story to several of us in the band one night on the bus. I had forgotten about it but evidently James A. Jr. divulged the time when him and his mom found out that his dad, James A. had been dealing drugs. He said they found one million dollars in cash hidden in the ceiling of their garage. He alleged it took thirteen hours to count it.

We had a long string of odd and bizarre incidents with bus drivers through the years. One wasn't who he said he was, several were on drugs, one was a theft and nearly all of them at one time or the other, fell asleep at the wheel. God surely protected us and kept us safe all those long and grueling miles.

The band had gotten so busy that we needed to bring on a dedicated road manager. Our soundman, Rusty was an incredible front of house technician, but he really didn't have the patience or the time to do all the things a road manager needed to do. Dealing with big productions and large sound systems was a full-time job.

Steve Navyac was a Godsend. When he came onboard things tightened up. He would do all the diligent scheduling for our shows and make sure everything was in order before we'd even get there. He'd call ahead and make sure we had hotel rooms and a person to take us back and forth to the venue. He also handled all of our personal issues like backstage passes, our meet and greets and made sure we had time to eat.

Before Steve it was a free-for-all. There were plenty of times where we'd forget to carve out time to put food in our mouths. Other times we'd show up and the motel rooms wouldn't be ready and we'd have to go on stage without a shower. Our manager, Christy could only do so much from Nashville. Putting out fires on the road was nearly impossible for him to do all the time. At least for now Steve had everything working the way it should.

Little Texas meeting Waylon Jennings
From left to right: Duane Propes, Dwayne O'Brien, Brady Seals, Waylon Jennings, Del Gray, Tim Rushow and Porter Howell
Photo Credit: Curtis Hilbun

What wasn't working was my internal compass. I had been drifting aimlessly for quite some time and didn't realize it. I didn't have a life other than the road life. While all the other guys in the band were dating and proposing, I was still hacking away at song titles and building pre-production tracks for our next record. I felt like a pressure cooker getting ready to pop the lid.

If my memory serves me right the band was out on the road three hundred and twenty-two days that year or it might've been the following year. I can't recall which magazine it was but they called us, "The hardest working band in Country Music". Now I don't know if that was true or not but I do know my body and mind were plumb worn out.

I tried to find a little comfort by spending time with girls on the road. There were a few that I liked but was never able to fully connect with them. There was one pretty girl in Tulsa that I liked but I eventually found out she was hanging out with every band that rolled into town. There was another who was a Dallas Cowboys cheerleader that ended up being a certified gold-digger.

While at home in Bellevue I received an anonymous letter warning me about her and her intentions with me. The letter writer said they had dated her in the past and she was seriously bad news. They went on to say that she had a safety deposit box full of money and jewelry from past boyfriends. When I confronted her about the letter and asked about the box, she flipped out. She started cussing and ranting on a scale that I had never heard before. I knew immediately that the letter had struck a nerve and I broke it off with her. Years later I found out that she had been with another big country star and tried to do some gold digging with him too.

I even tried getting back with Roxane. I flew her out to see me while I was playing in Fort Worth, Texas. It had been five or six years since I had seen her. I was looking forward to seeing what she looked like. When I finally did see her, she was still as pretty as ever but she had dyed her hair red. Nothing against redheads, but she didn't look like the Roxane I remembered. We hung out for a day or two but something was off. We tried to reignite the old flame, but for some reason the feeling wasn't there like it had been before.

After one of the many times playing Fort Worth, we headed down to Austin. We were scheduled to perform at a giant nightclub called, Dance Across Texas. But the night before Richard Perna, who was the head honcho at our publishing company wanted to take all of us to a club. He was wanting to celebrate O'Brien's wedding that was just around the bend. Dwayne had met a woman named DeLisa and they had fallen completely in love. They had been dating for years and it was time for him to tie the knot.

That night we saw a lot of pretty ladies there and Porter and I heard our manager Christy say the phrase "God bless 'em!" Well the next day at soundcheck Porter came over to my keyboard and said, "What do you think about the title "God Blessed Texas?" I loved it! I knew exactly where he wanted to take it and knew it would be easy and fun to write.

After we finished checking our mics and levels, we all headed back to the motel. Porter and I were fixated on getting some lyrics started so we agreed to meet down at the pool and work on it. There wasn't a guitar around but that didn't stop us, we were just rappin' the words and phrases and kinda knew where it was headed musically. For the next six months we tried going to O'Brien and to our songwriter friend, Jay Booker, to see if they wanted to write it with us. Neither of them ever really thought much of the song idea, so they passed.

Finally, Christy made Porter and me finish it. He had heard bits and pieces of it and thought there might be something to the song. The tune had been sitting idle for too long. Porter and I finished it in a motel room somewhere out west and we brought it to the band to see what they thought. I remember workin' it up at soundcheck at some outdoor stage. That day our booking agent, Ron Baird came to our soundcheck. Christy told me that Ron freaked out when he heard it and thought the song was going to be a big ginormous hit.

Warner Brothers released our first single off our new album, *Big Time* on May 13th, 1993. The band had been anticipating it for quite some time and we knew it was do or die time. We felt like we had recorded the best music we had at the time and it was finally up to the public to see what they thought.

Our first single was, "What Might Have Been". I don't remember why they went with that single but whoever chose it, chose right. The song got traction right off the bat. Radio stations all over the country started playing it. We also simultaneously released a video to all of the country video channels like CMT, TNN and GAC.

A portion of the video was filmed in sepia tone and it focused around World War II. It showed a couple dancing just before the soldier has to go off to war. The second part was a full storyline about a guy named Michael that has a son named Tommy. It shows them visiting Michael's grandfather, Nathan, who lives in a nursing home. The little boy, Tommy shows his great-grandfather a picture that he had found of Nathan and a woman he met during World War II, named Clarice.

During the visit, Tommy's grandfather tells Tommy more about Clarice and about how they had lost contact with each other after the war ended. After Michael and Tommy leave, Nathan is shown walking around the nursing home when all of a sudden, he passes an elderly woman. He stops and turns around to see if the woman looks familiar. It turns out that it's his long-lost love, Clarice.

When I saw the final cut of the video I was blown away. I had no idea that the storyline had been filmed at all. The band only experienced being filmed on a big electronic lazy Susan where we kept spinning around and around, singing the song. Once I saw the video of us and the added footage, I knew the song was going to be at least a top ten single.

The song exceeded all of our expectations. It went on to be our first number one song on the country charts. It even showed up on the Adult Contemporary and Pop charts. I'll never forget hearing it on the radio for the first time. Tim and I were driving his little white Mazda RX7 around a big curve on a Dallas freeway. Both of us flipped out. It sounded amazing coming through his car speakers. I remember us both talking about how it could be the song to send us to the top.

Fruit Of The World

There are so many ways that we are tempted by the fruits of the world. Drugs, money, sex...the list goes on and on. For me, I gave into those temptations...I was genuinely adrift, even if I didn't necessarily realize it at the time. I allowed myself to get lost in the everyday grind and the superficial temptations. I didn't think much about my walk with God. But I'm not alone. The Bible is full of stories of people that gave into sinful desires, just as I did.

* Samson was enticed by Delilah and that deception led to his death. -Judges 16-18
* King David committed adultery with Bathsheba. -2 Samuel 11-12
* And we all know what happened with Eve in the Garden of Eden. -Genesis 3

Being tempted does not make us a bad person. Heck, even Jesus was tempted! Luke 4:1-2. What really matters is how we react when tempted. One way to fight temptation is by focusing on something else, things that are good and pure. *"Finally, brethren, whatsoever things are true, whatsoever things are honest, whatsoever things are just, whatsoever things are pure, whatsoever things are lovely, whatsoever things are of good report; if there be any virtue, and if there be any praise, think on these things." -Philippians 4:8 KJV*

Temptation becomes bad as soon as we say yes to it when we should've said no. Thankfully, we have a Father that forgives. *"If we confess our sins, he is faithful and just to*

forgive us our sins, and to cleanse us from all unrighteousness."
-John 1:9 KJV

That doesn't mean that we should keep giving into sin though. When we do, we start to backslide just like I mentioned in the first chapter of this book. We need to be aware of exactly who is tempting us, Satan. It's certainly not God. *"Let no man say when he is tempted, I am tempted of God: for God cannot be tempted with evil, neither tempteth he any man: But every man is tempted, when he is drawn away of his own lust, and enticed. Then when lust hath conceived, it bringeth forth sin: and sin, when it is finished, bringeth forth death." -James 1:13-15 KJV*

To help us not sin, we need to think about the consequences of giving into it. There can be physical, emotional and spiritual harm when doing so. Praying will battle temptation. Jesus said: *"Watch and pray, that ye enter not into temptation: the spirit indeed is willing, but the flesh is weak." -Matthew 26:41 KJV*

"Blessed is the man that endureth temptation: for when he is tried, he shall receive the crown of life, which the Lord hath promised to them that love him." -James 1:12 KJV

Chapter Three:
The Sunset House

*"May he give you the desire of your heart
and make all your plans succeed." -Psalm 20:4 NIV*

From the late 1970s to the early '90s there was a hit television show on CBS called *Dallas*. It was essentially a soap opera that centered around a family that owned a large ranch in Texas called Southfork Ranch. The property where the series was filmed was located about twenty-five miles north of the real Dallas. That's where we filmed the video for "God Blessed Texas."

The concept was thought of by director Gerry Wenner. The main portion of the video shows the band set up at the front entrance of the ranch performing the song. He also had a group of beautiful girls there too for B-roll footage. We sat around sipping on drinks by a huge pool that was located on the grounds, with girls in bikinis walking all around us.

Again, I had no idea that Gerry had spent other days filming other scenes for the video. He had even filmed the Dallas Cowboy Cheerleaders on the football field dancing to the song. There's no telling how much time and money was spent shooting all the footage.

God Blessed Texas Video Shoot at Southfork Ranch-
Parker, Texas
From left to right: Duane Propes, Brady Seals, Tim Rushlow,
Dwayne O'Brien and Del Gray
Photo Credit: Steve Navyac

God Blessed Texas Video Shoot at Southfork Ranch-
Parker, Texas
Gerry Wenner director and his crew and Little Texas
Photo Credit: Steve Navyac

God Blessed Texas Video Shoot at Southfork Ranch-
Parker, Texas
Brady Seals
Photo Credit: Erin and Carin Purdom

We released the song and video on July 17th,1993.
We had just come off the success of "What Might Have
Been," and we knew this single had to be a strong one.
We were all a little nervous though because of the
overtly Texas themed content. We were worried that
radio stations in places like Lexington, Kentucky or
Tucson, Arizona wouldn't even play a song about Texas.
However, we felt that if the Beach Boys had a hit song
about "California Girls," then why couldn't we have one
about Texas girls. It was a risk we were willing to take.

We had been playing the song live and the feedback
from the crowd was always positive no matter where we
played it. We started closing our shows with it. We'd play
the first nine notes of the college anthem, "The Eyes of
Texas" at the beginning of the song each night just to
work up the crowd.

During a small break in the schedule I went home to visit my parents in Ohio. I was exhausted and didn't know which way was up. Anxiety was creeping in without even realizing it. I was starting to not sleep well at night and I was drinking antacid medicine, Maalox, every day to settle my stomach.

One day while trying to calm down, I got a call from Christy asking if I could come back to Nashville and record a song for an Eagles tribute record. Warner Bros. was going to release it and have some of their artists record their own versions of Eagles hits.

I had mixed feelings about it. I was a huge Eagles fan and I felt that recording one of their songs would be too much like walking on sacred ground. Christy also didn't know which artists on the label would be a part of it.

I was so tired during that time and I had just settled in for three or four days to visit with my mom and dad. I really didn't want to make the trip to Nashville and possibly be a part of a project that might turn out cheesy. I said no. I told Christy to go ahead and record the tune without me.

The guys recorded "Peaceful Easy Feeling" and O'Brien sang it. When I heard the final mix, I was blown away. He sounded great and I loved the tracks Porter laid down on the recording. The harmonies sounded fantastic!

After I got back out on the road with them, they told me that Travis Tritt had recorded "Take It Easy." Travis had asked the guys in The Eagles if they'd make an appearance in his video and they said yes. Don Henley,

Glenn Frey, Don Felder and Timothy B. Schmidt were all there. The Eagles had split up, acrimoniously in 1980, with Henley famously saying the band would get back together "when hell freezes over."

Frey had been reluctant up to that point to join back up with the band. Once the video shoot had happened and he met with Henley they talked about a reunion. Frey was quoted, *"After years passed, you really sort of remember that you were friends first ... I just remembered how much we genuinely had liked each other and how much fun we'd had."*

I had no idea when I turned down playing on that record it would turn out to be a monumental musical event. Looking back, I know it was a bad decision on my part. The record was titled, *Common Thread: Songs of The Eagles*. If I'm not mistaken it ultimately sold over three million albums. The record and video were the impetus for the Eagles getting back together for the mega-successful *Hell Freezes Over* tour.

The coolest part of performing "Peaceful Easy Feeling," was when we got the chance to play the song months later live in Nashville on TNN. We were backstage warming up before the show singing another Eagles song, "Seven Bridges Road," when Don Henley poked his head in our dressing room and said, "Sounds familiar!" We all fell out! We had no idea he was listening to us on the other side of the door. Evidently, he was supposed to be on the show as well to talk about his experience of being a part of the Eagles tribute record.

At the time I only had one or two artists that I really wanted to meet in my lifetime. One was Don Henley, the other was Paul McCartney. I had just checked off one and he was as nice as he could be.

We had just gotten off the road touring with Clint Black on his *Hard Way* tour when CAA secured another large package tour for us. We were scheduled to open the show for Travis Tritt and Trisha Yearwood. It was called the Rock 'n Country tour, sponsored by Budweiser.

The tour hit major towns all across America. We mainly played in large amphitheaters and stadiums and the crowds went wild. Travis really did it up right. The sound and lighting rigs were top of the line. He also had large screens on each side of the stage and had a video production team filming every angle possible.

Ken Kragen, Travis and Trisha's manager brought in a guy named Joe Layton to coordinate everyone's nightly performances. Joe was a highly successful Broadway choreographer that had won an Emmy Award and a Tony Award in the past. He had also directed and produced shows for Paul Lynde, Hal Linden, Richard Pryor and Olivia Newton-John. He had also worked on specials starring Cher, The Carpenters, Diana Ross, Dolly Parton, Carol Burnett and Willie Nelson. We had never worked with someone before for staging and choreography, but Joe made it fun.

He gave us his suggestions about which songs to put in our set-list and where to put them in the running order. He even offered up his opinion on cutting certain sections out of songs, so they would be more powerful. Everything he suggested was minimal but very effective. No wonder he was an award winner.

Rock 'n Country Tour 1993
From left to right: Travis Tritt, Dwayne O'Brien, Porter Howell,
Duane Propes, Tim Rushlow, Brady Seals and Del Gray

He also recommended that at the end of each night, all three acts do something special together on stage. Travis chose a Hank Williams Jr. song called "We Are Young Country," to make that happen. Each artist sang lyrics from the song and it made for a superb way to end the show. Sadly, a short time after working with us, Joe passed away in his home in Florida.

One night is still etched in my mind where I came to the stage for the last song and everyone was just standing around. They said that Travis was going to just rock out for a while and play some classic southern rock songs instead. I just stood there with the guys from Little Texas and listened to Tritt rattle off some Marshall Tucker and Bob Seger tunes.

After he got done with the next song, he waved for us all to come out on stage with him. I turned to the guys and nodded and started to walk out there with him. I thought for sure they were going to follow since we had all made eye contact. I walked halfway to Travis then looked around and the guys weren't there. They didn't follow me!

There I was, all alone in front of a stadium full of people by myself with Travis and his band. I had no idea what I was supposed to do. He whispered in my ear, "You take the verses and I sing the chorus." I was like a deer caught in the headlights. I could hear the band vamping the signature lick for Lynyrd Skynyrd's song, "Call Me the Breeze". I was familiar with it but certainly didn't know the lyrics to the verses.

I yelled back over the distorted guitars, "I DON'T KNOW THE LYRICS ON THE VERSES, CAN I SING THE CHORUS?" I didn't even know if he heard me and I thought my heart was going to beat out of my chest. Luckily, Travis realized I didn't know what I was doing and he stepped up and started singing the first verse. I winged it when the chorus came around and just sang harmony with him. It was crazy! I couldn't believe the guys of Little Texas left me hanging out there alone. We all laughed about it later.

That year of the Rock 'n Country Tour was truly insane. Little Texas had become friends with the rock band Firehouse. I remember hanging out on a houseboat on some lake somewhere and having a ball. We also got to hang out with Bret Michaels from Poison out in LA. I can't recall too many of the details, other than we got to listen to some music he was writing in the studio.

We also got to visit the White House. We had gotten a call to fill in for the band Take 6. They were supposed to perform with Kenny G and Whitney Houston and had something come up where they couldn't do it. I thought we were an odd replacement, but we did it anyway. We met Vice President Al Gore and toured the White House. I guess Bill was off somewhere running the country. I still have a picture of me sitting at the Steinway grand piano in the East Room that Harry Truman and Richard Nixon had played.

Touring the White House
Brady Seals
Photo Credit: Steve Navyac

Touring the White House
Porter Howell and Brady Seals
Photo Credit: Steve Navyac

Touring the White House
From left to right: Tim Rushlow, Porter Howell, Brady Seals,
Kenny G, Del Gray and Dwayne O'Brien
Photo Credit: Steve Navyac

Little Texas meeting Vice President Al Gore
From left to right: Brady Seals, Al Gore, Del Gray, Porter Howell,
Dwayne O'Brien and Tim Rushlow

Right after releasing "God Blessed Texas" the label chose "My Love" to be the next single. I couldn't believe it. I was thrilled to death but nervous. We had just had two number one songs and I didn't want the song I sang to ruin our streak. I was told that we were going to film the video on Grand Cayman Island. I even got to pick out the girl that was going to co-star in it with me.

Gerry Wenner, the same guy who directed "God Blessed Texas," was chosen to direct it. We all met to talk about the concept and he said he imagined it looking like the old 1953 Academy Award winning film, *From Here to Eternity*. He thought it would be cool to shoot the video in black and white.

I went along with whatever Gerry and the record label suggested. When they decided that it was really going to happen, I started working out like Arnold Schwarzenegger. I knew I was going to be half naked rolling around on a beach with a beautiful woman. I spent every spare moment of each day training and eating right.

My new friend Jeff that played for Clint Black suggested a workout routine to get in shape. He suggested that I even shave all the hair off my body, just like bodybuilders do, to look ripped on the beach. Reluctantly, I did.

We headed down to the island in December of '93. I remember the first time I saw Sue Laguna in person, the girl that was going to be my lover in the video. She was gorgeous and had beautiful eyes. I had picked her out from several different models to play opposite me. I knew she'd be perfect for the video.

Sue was so kind and professional during the whole shoot. There was never a romantic connection behind the scenes even though we got along wonderfully. When it came time for the beach scene, we agreed not to touch lips on camera. We felt the anticipation would be a nice element. We spent the next five days shooting scenes on the beach and swimming with the stingrays at Stingray City. I had been there years before while I had been in the 50s band, The Varsities and to be back there again felt great.

Little Texas, Sue and the film crew stayed at a hotel right by the beach called, The Sunset House. That's where Sue filmed all of the close-up shots of her underneath the waterfall. The waterfall was right there in the hotel pool.

My Love Video Shoot- Grand Cayman
From left to right: Sue Laguna, Brady Seals, Gerry Wenner
Photo Credit: Christy DiNapoli

My Love Video Shoot- Grand Cayman
From left to right: Debra Wingo (makeup), Sue Laguna and Brady Seals
Photo Credit: Christy DiNapoli

Our friend at Warner Bros., Gene Dries facilitated the whole experience. He arranged and coordinated the Cayman Island visit from free rooms and diving at Sunset House as well as securing a number of other freebies from other businesses and the government.

All he asked for in return was a "product shot" somewhere in the video. At the last-minute Gerry, the director wasn't thrilled about putting logos in the video but thanks to Christy interceding, he showed the Sunset House logo on the seawall in the final cut. You can also see scenes in the video of Sue and me at Smith's Cove, Seven Mile Beach and the abandoned set on the North Sound used by the movie, The Firm.

The only time the whole band was shown was at the very end of the video. It's an unforgettable silhouette shot of us on the rocks of the beach. Gerry made us appear bigger than life.

The single was released in January of 1994 and "My Love" went on to be our third number one song. It soared to the top of the chart on April the 2nd and stayed at number one for two weeks. It was our only number one song on the Billboard chart. The two singles before it had not reached number one on there but they did reach the top spot on the R&R (Radio & Records) chart. The video also received CMA's Video of The Year award that year.

As part of the coverage of the video shoot, the television show *Entertainment Tonight* came down and covered the making of the video as well, a day of scuba diving with the band while Sue and I were engaging in "skin, sun and sand". I was told later that the ET video piece was the longest music related segment that they ran in 1994.

The band performed an unplugged set on the deck at a place called, My Bar that was taped by ET and we performed "What Might Have Been" as the play out music for the episode.

Before the single had been released, I had promised myself that if "My Love" went to number one, I would buy myself a Harley. I had always wanted one even though my dad had told the story of him almost dying on one back in the '60s.

Sure enough, I went over to the Harley Davidson dealership off White Bridge Road in Nashville and picked out a grey and white Heritage Softail Special. I remember getting it in the winter time and it was freezing outside. I called my friend Greg who had a Harley too and we went for a ride that day anyway. I didn't even have my motorcycle license yet, but it didn't hold me back. I had to do it. I about froze myself to death but that didn't stop me from celebrating another one of God's blessings.

I hadn't owned my own bike since I was a kid. Dad had bought me a little yellow Suzuki RM80 when I was about thirteen years old. It felt good to get in the wind again. It also felt good to have three number one songs in a row. I'd go on to win ASCAP's Triple Play Award that year.

The boys and I were appearing on shows like the nationally syndicated show *Live with Regis and Kathie Lee* and all of The Nashville Network shows. We were invited to plug in and play at the Grand Ole Opry several times too and got to hang out backstage with The King of Country Music, Roy Acuff and The Possum, George

Jones. I met artists such as Dolly Parton, Waylon Jennings, Billy Gibbons (ZZ Top), Merle Haggard, Ginger Baker (Cream) and so many more that I can't even recall.

Little Texas meeting Ginger Baker
From left to right: Porter Howell, Brady Seals, Dwayne O'Brien, Ginger Baker, Del Gray, Duane Propes, Tim Rushlow

I was dumbfounded by all the opportunities that were coming my way. I was also able to shake hands for the first time with my relative, Dan Seals, not long before he passed away. He was one of the most gentle human beings I've ever come in contact with.

I kept writing non-stop and I was recording demos as fast I could. Porter and I had come up with a song that we thought was in the same vein as "God Blessed Texas" called "Kick A Little" and we were hoping it would catapult us to the top once again. The band had been in the studio every chance we could recording our next project that would come out after *Big Time*.

Chapter Three: The Sunset House

We felt like we had a good set of songs that were just a little deeper and had more substance than our last record and we certainly felt like we were maturing as a band. We had also taken some really cool pictures for the CD cover up in New York after receiving a handsome budget to go shopping for new clothes. We ended the trip with a traditional Italian meal at a little place on Mulberry Street called La Mela. That was some of the best food I've ever eaten!

Hamstein Music had set up a writing appointment for me with a guy named, Stephen Allen Davis at my home in Bellevue. I had been told that Stephen had written Percy Sledge's song, "Take Time to Know Her" when he was just a kid. I was impressed and couldn't wait to set in on a tune.

He came in that day and had the title, "Amy's Back In Austin" and I loved it. He told me that he had visited a place in Austin called La Zona Rosa Cafe and loved the name of the restaurant and thought it would be a good name for a song. He later changed it to "Amy's Back In Austin" and thankfully he did. It went on to be a top five single for us on the charts and the video was nominated for a GRAMMY.

The other song on that record that really stood out for me was "Redneck Like Me". It was one that I sang lead on. Our co-writing friend, Jay Booker wrote it by himself. Jay had come out on the road once or twice with us to see if we could write together. We weren't able to co-write anything that made it on the CD but I remember him playing the redneck song, and I loved it the way that it was.

Ultimately, we finished the CD and turned it into Warner Bros. I had written eight out of the ten songs that made the cut. The other two songs were Jay's song, "Redneck Like Me" and "Your Days Are Numbered" written by Porter and O'Brien. It had been a long tedious year gathering all of the material needed to make it happen. I was glad it was over. Luckily there was time to breathe and let loose for a while.

BLESSINGS EVEN IN SIN

God never ceases to amaze me. He blesses us even when we sin! I was having one-night stands and smoking pot every other night. My ego was out of hand and was caught up in greed and worldly possessions.

Look at King David again. David was a believer but he kept committing sins. And what did God do? He continued to love and be there for him. Ultimately David was punished for his sins but the punishment was just, and came from love. Hebrews 12:6 NIV says, *"because the Lord disciplines the one he loves, and he chastens everyone he accepts as his son."*

But he still blesses us. I know he still blessed me when I was living my life in sin. He continued to give me songs to have good income, accolades and let me see the world. He didn't have to do that. Just like he didn't have to be there for David. God could have easily ended David's life or mine with a snap of a finger. But instead He helped David and me up. He guided me like the Shepherd that He is. He would eventually lead me to a better and more uncontaminated life. Thankfully, we have a merciful God.

The Bible also teaches that we may not be blessed while sinning as well. "*Wherefore the Lord God of Israel saith, I said indeed that thy house, and the house of thy father, should walk before me forever: but now the Lord saith, Be it far from me; for them that honour me I will honour, and they that despise me shall be lightly esteemed.*" -1 Samuel 2:30 KJV

The wise thing to do is honor God and stay in His Word and obey it. "*And it shall come to pass, if thou shalt hearken diligently unto the voice of the Lord thy God, to observe and to do all his commandments which I command thee this day, that the Lord thy God will set thee on high above all nations of the earth:*

And all these blessings shall come on thee, and overtake thee, if thou shalt hearken unto the voice of the Lord thy God. Blessed shalt thou be in the city, and blessed shalt thou be in the field." -Deuteronomy 28: 1-3 KJV

The good news is God has big blessings for all of us! His blessings can come in differing forms, at various times, under all types of circumstances, and from a multitude of sources. He desires to give all of them to us.

"*Go and proclaim these words toward the north, and say, Return, thou backsliding Israel, saith the Lord; and I will not cause mine anger to fall upon you: for I am merciful, saith the Lord, and I will not keep anger for ever.*" -Jerimiah 3:12 KJV

CHAPTER FOUR:
THE DARK NIGHT

"When thou passest through the waters, I will be with thee; and through the rivers, they shall not overflow thee: when thou walkest through the fire, thou shalt not be burned; neither shall the flame kindle upon thee." -Isaiah 43:2 KJV

The band kept attending one party or awards show after another. I couldn't keep up with them. There was one small gathering that was thrown in the basement of an upscale restaurant in Nashville called Mere Bulles. The band, our crew, management and record label executives were there. I don't remember the reason, but I do remember seeing a beautiful dark-haired waitress serving us drinks and my jaw dropping to the floor. The guys kept hounding me to ask her out that night and before I left, I did.

We became an item for years to come. Her name was Tiffany Jones. Tiffany was a Christian and had moved to Nashville from Mississippi. She had been a swimsuit model several years before I met her. She also had a love for music and could really sing, but never pursued it professionally. Every second I wasn't touring, writing or recording, I spent with her. I fell in love and for the first time in my life, I could see myself putting a ring on someone's finger.

Chapter Four: The Dark Night

Stepping onto the bus after being wrapped up in her arms got harder and harder to do. Thankfully, we had been told we had two or three months off before our next big tour. The band was scheduled to co-headline a tour with a new hat act named Tim McGraw. I met Tim before in the recording studio with Tommy Barnes. Tommy knew Tim because he wrote his single "Indian Outlaw." I remember hanging out with Tim and thinking, "Bless your heart, you have no idea how hard it's going to be to make it in this crazy business."

When we were first asked by CAA about co-headlining a tour with McGraw, I knew it would be a good bill, even though we had several more hits than he did. After seeing Tim's video for his second single, "Don't Take The Girl," I knew he would sky rocket to the top. The song was too good and he delivered it superbly. Co-headlining was the right call for sure. I felt then that following him on stage would get harder and harder as the months rolled by.

I was hopeful in my life during that time. I was in love and I knew that I was going to have time off soon to spend it with Tiffany. I planned on vacationing with her and clearing my hazy head. I had also started reading The Bible from front to back in my bunk at night, in a quest to find peace in my life. I stopped smoking pot and hanging out with random girls after shows. I even tried to quit cursing and being so negative in general.

I was also feeling the guilt of sleeping with girls I didn't know. I remember inviting them back to my hotel room and just shaking inside while I was with them. I'd have to turn on the heating unit really high to try to stop my body from trembling. I worried myself to death thinking maybe I had caught some sort of sexually transmitted disease like AIDS or syphilis. I was a mess. It was an absolute low point in my life.

I knew it was time to turn my life around. I couldn't take it anymore. The Holy Spirit was tugging me every day and night. I had to set my sights on finding the shore after being at the mercy of the devil's current for years. No one was going to stop me either! I had spent too many late nights partying on the bus, breaking young girls' hearts and turning my back on God. Deep down in my soul I knew what was right. It was time to follow God's Word and let Him lead me home.

Just as the hope of spending time at home was cresting, we got news that Christy and our booking agent had accepted a Fair tour instead. I remember Porter walking on the bus and breaking the news to everyone. We were now going to be playing county fairs and smelling corn dogs and funnel cakes instead of spending time with those we love.

I was devastated. It was as if something inside me broke. All of the guys had been so excited about having down time to cool off and now we'd be thrown right back into the fire. The guys had been talking about where they were going to get away and now, we were scrambling to call our families to let them know about the change in plans. It was tough.

Meanwhile I was brooding. I was sick of living my life on someone else's clock. For eight years I had been living out of a suitcase and having to be where someone else told me to be. I was at my limit.

I told Porter to ask Christy if there's any way we could get out of doing the new dates. He resisted and said we just need to suck it up and make it happen. What he didn't realize was, I was already past my limit. The guys knew I was mad. I kept saying, "I can't believe this!, you all were wanting time off too! This isn't fair y'all!" I finally said, "I can't do it guys, I'm sorry; but this isn't cool!"

They were angry, just like me but as soon as I said, "I can't do it," the band turned on me. No one was on my side anymore. They all agreed that if Christy booked the shows, we had to do them, no matter what. I stuck by my guns though. I wasn't going to budge this time and they knew it. Christy and CAA worked for us, not the other way around.

Several of the guys were nice and tried to calm me down and talk me into doing the shows but it didn't work. I was too far gone. I just didn't think it was right that Christy would book the shows after he had told us we were going to have time off. He didn't talk it over with us at all. I really needed the break. I wasn't able to stress it to them enough.

For the next several days the guys were mad at me. It made it hard to be out there when the whole band had turned against me. I felt like an outsider, the antagonist. I hated for them to be mad at me but I knew I had to stand my ground. My body was telling me the same thing.

And that's when I had to show up for the filming of the second version of the video for "Kick A Little". Yes, we shot two videos. The director was Jon Small. Jon was a big shot video director and producer who had directed the Run-DMC/ Aerosmith video for "Walk This Way," that was so popular in the '80s. He had worked with plenty of other artists too. After filming our first version of the video down in Atlanta weeks before, we were told that Jon said someone stole the film out of his car while he was in New York, editing the video.

We were all flabbergasted as to why anyone would want to steal film out of someone's car. The excuse was a little sketchy but we just went with it. We knew the video needed to be done ASAP, so we re-scheduled it at the Tennessee Performing Arts Center in Nashville.

Just so I don't have to relive it for the third time, here's how the Wikipedia website explains the concept of the video: *The video starts with a shot of storm clouds. It then cuts to an unnamed actor in a red cap, parking his Volkswagen Bug and saying "Man, it's like there's a storm growing there!" as a flash of lightning appears. As the song starts, it shows the band performing live on an empty stage, while being bombarded with debris. During the guitar solo, a really strong tornado and heavy windstorm breaks down the door to meet the band and the unnamed actor, with a rubber chicken, on stage, where the band continues performing while being bombarded with even more debris. As the song ends, another unnamed actor says "Man, that Texas twister sho' can kick!" as debris got blown up in the air from him kicking his foot, which then goes into a reprise of the song's guitar riff.*

The making of that version was excruciating for me. I barely talked to the guys. They didn't talk to me either. I remember sitting out in the theatre seats with Christy telling him my side of the story. It didn't matter what I said, he had already started signing contracts for the fair dates. I was between a rock and a hard place. I didn't know what to do and I started to freak out.

Chapter Four: The Dark Night

1994 proved to be the best and worst year ever for Little Texas. The best part was, we had three songs on the Billboard Country chart at the same time with three different singers. O'Brien fronted the band on "Peaceful Easy Feeling", I was singing "My Love" and we had just released "Kick A Little" with Tim singing lead. That had never happened before in country music and might not ever happen again. The worst part was about to come. I would leave the band.

I remember exactly how the beginning of the end happened. The band had played the Grand Ole Opry and we were backstage meeting some fans when I felt like the walls were closing in. I had never fainted in my life but I felt like I might. I started to sweat heavily. I thought that I was going to throw up. I excused myself from the meet and greet line and went over to Tiffany and said, "Something's wrong, let's go...and can you drive?" I let the guys know I was leaving and off we went.

The thirty-minute drive felt like two hours. I crawled up like a ball in the seat, extremely nauseated. When we arrived back at the house, she helped me to the bedroom but I couldn't make it to the bed. I just fell to the floor and tried not to vomit. She tried everything to help the situation, but nothing worked.

Several times I thought about going to the ER but just thought I had some sort of stomach bug or maybe even the flu. I held out through the night and eventually worked my way up to the bed. I laid there the next day but didn't get any better. I came to the conclusion that I need to call my doctor to have them do some tests.

All of the tests came back negative but when I told the doctor I had been very stressed lately, he said, "Brady, I think you're going through a major crisis and you probably need to rest for a few weeks." I knew that would go over like a lead balloon with the band. They'd never agree to that.

The doctor also recommended that I go see an internist. He thought it would be best to have a specialist do some tests about the stomach issues I was having. Luckily, I was able to see one the next day and I had Tiffany drive me there. I told the doctor that I had always had a nervous stomach. I told him that I had an upper GI test done when I was a kid because my stomach would hurt. I thought maybe there was some sort of correlation.

After he ran a few tests he believed my stomach was generating too much acid due to anxiety and stress. He recommended bed rest and for me and to see a psychiatrist. He also prescribed some medication to keep the acid from coming up in my esophagus and sent me home.

The bus was supposed to leave in a couple of days and I didn't know what to do, so I called Christy. I explained what I had just been through and he sounded suspicious on the phone. Looking back, I don't blame him. I probably would've been too.

You see, for about a week now I had been saying to Christy and the guys that I wasn't going to go out on the next tour. Now I was saying that I can't go out on the next weekend run! Christy was mad but I was immobile. There was nothing I could do. I literally had a hard time getting out of bed. The room would spin every time

I moved my head. I thought I was having a good old-fashioned nervous breakdown.

I can only imagine the conversation that he had with Porter. I'm sure the guys were fuming when they heard the news. The problem was, I was too sick to care. I felt like the world was coming to an end. I started imagining the possibility of losing my job, for me feeling like this the rest of my life and something diabolical was at work in my head.

Reluctantly, I called my Mom and Dad and told them what was going on. They got in Dad's truck that morning and were in Bellevue that night. Having them there made it a little better. Mom fixed some homemade food for me and would sometimes lay in the bed with me and pray.

I grew up believing that the devil was real and Mom and I both agreed that the devil was attacking. I had told her that I had been reading The Bible and trying to live a better life and she wholeheartedly thought Satan was trying his best to torment me with fear.

Meanwhile the guys went out on the run without me. They just told the fans that I had a stomach issue and I'd be back soon. I think they played two weeks' worth of shows without me singing and playing keyboards.

Back at home I wasn't any better. I didn't want to, but I went to see a psychiatrist. He listened to my story for two hours and diagnosed me as having a panic disorder and depression. I was like, "I have what?" I had never heard of a panic disorder up to that point in my life and I had never considered myself depressed. I had always been a worrier throughout my life about little things like germs and had a nervous stomach as a teenager, but never imagined a panic disorder or depression.

I had also been an outgoing and confident kid. This diagnosis was hard for me to swallow but I had to go with what the doctor claimed. He prescribed the antidepressant, Prozac.

That week after taking the medicine he prescribed was one of the hardest weeks ever. Prozac had major side effects on me. My body would randomly twitch to the point where I'd spill a glass of water. My neck would twitch too and it scared me to no end. I felt like I was dying. I also couldn't sleep. I'd stay up all hours of the night trying to watch TV and pray.

My mom suggested that I have my pastor from Ohio come down and pray for me and I had no objections. I'd do anything at this stage to stop the madness. To this day I'm thankful for John Carter Jr. and my brother Greg for coming down just to pray for me. I could feel the Holy Spirit that day and it comforted me. They too believed that I was going through a spiritual warfare and gave me some verses in The Bible to refer to when I started feeling down or fearful.

My mom had also called my former boss, Sandy Powell and her manager and husband Jim Prater to come over and pray as well. They sat on the couch and listened to me explain my situation and were so supportive and kind. I knew that God was with me. Those praying sessions gave me hope that things would eventually turn around.

Insomnia was making me irritable and concerned, so I called my doctor to let him know. I also let him know about the sporadic twitching. He prescribed Elavil for me to take at night. He said it would relax me and make me sleepy. He also advised that if the twitching didn't stop in the next five days to call him and he'd prescribe something different.

It never stopped! In fact, it got worse. However, the Elavil did seem to work and I was able to get five or six hours of sleep at night. The Prozac wasn't working for me. I was terribly nauseated. I'd spend hours on the floor of the bathroom feeling dizzy and sweaty.

Time seemed to drag on during that month. I read The Bible every chance I could and I would only watch positive stuff on TV. I was down though, really down. I remember one day sitting on the side of the bed when no one was around and thinking that maybe I should just end it all.

I had a nine-millimeter handgun in my nightstand and for a moment I thought about taking my life. I felt like such a hindrance to everyone. I didn't want to be looked at as weak and pathetic anymore. I couldn't stand what I had become.

But as soon as the thought came to me, it was gone. I knew that suicide wasn't the answer. God was with me in that moment and brought me clarity when I needed it the most. I had reached the bottom and I knew deep inside that things were going to get better from that moment on.

I had grown so weary and I had lost a lot of weight from not being able to eat. I just wanted God to take me out of this nightmare. I had heard from a friend or family member about a poem from the sixteenth century written by a Spanish Monk named Saint John of the Cross. His writings were supposedly about the soul's journey from the distractions and entanglements of the world to the perfect peace and harmony of God. According to the poet, the "dark night of the soul" is synonymous with traveling the "narrow way" that Jesus spoke of in The Bible in Matthew 7:13-14 KJV. "*Enter ye in at the strait gate: for wide is the gate, and broad is the way, that leadeth to destruction, and many there be which go in thereat: Because strait is the gate, and narrow is the way, which leadeth unto life, and few there be that find it.*"

I found the poem so incredibly comforting to know that I wasn't the only one going through a hopeless time of my life. The "narrow way" wasn't the easiest way but it was the right way. It also made me realize that through the ages people have been going through the same kind of depression and suffering as me. The monk wrote that the experience was about testing. The journeyman or woman goes through agony, confusion, fear, and uncertainty including doubts of God. But on the other side is union with God and you will feel God's glory and serenity.

WHY DO WE SUFFER?

Job was the biblical guy that I most felt a connection with during my dark night of the soul. I had read his story in The Bible when I was a kid but after what I went through, I had a deeper appreciation of his dreadful account. It also made me ask a lot of questions though. Questions like, why do people suffer? And where is God in the suffering?

The book of Job begins by describing him as a just and righteous man. But Satan comes before the Lord and God allows him to test Job. Unthinkable misfortune befalls Job and his faithfulness is gauged by three different conversations with his friends and family. Job passes the tests in the end and God rewards him giving him greater happiness than he ever had before.

"The Lord blessed the latter part of Job's life more than the former part. He had fourteen thousand sheep, six thousand camels, a thousand yoke of oxen and a thousand donkeys. And he also had seven sons and three daughters. The first daughter he named Jemimah, *the second Keziah and the third Keren-Happuch. Nowhere in all the land were there found women as beautiful as Job's daughters, and their father granted them an inheritance along with their brothers. After this, Job lived a hundred and forty years; he saw his children and their children to the fourth generation. And so Job died, an old man and full of years." -Job 42:12-17 NIV*

The questions about why we suffer and where God is during the suffering was not that easy to answer. I do know that he restores and blesses us when it's all said and done.

"And not only so, but we glory in tribulations also: knowing that tribulation worketh patience; And patience, experience; and experience, hope." -Romans 5:3-4 KJV

"But and if ye suffer for righteousness' sake, happy are ye: and be not afraid of their terror, neither be troubled" -1 Peter 3:14 KJV

I have also come to realize that God is God and He doesn't need to answer to anyone about why. Instead we need to see His wonders of creation and need to try to comprehend just how small we really are in the scheme of things. God's wisdom is beyond our comprehension and why He does what He does is unfathomable.

"For as the heavens are higher than the earth, so are my ways higher than your ways, and my thoughts than your thoughts."
-Isaiah 55:9 KJV

Chapter Five:
Hardly On A Harley

"He maketh me to lie down in green pastures: he leadeth me beside the still waters." -Psalm 23:2 KJV

Tiffany was an angel during those months. She stayed with me when she didn't have to. She took care of me in the middle of the night and would hold me when I had trembling fits. Her devotion made me fall deeper in love with her. Between her, my parents, my family and close friends I was able to slowly crawl out of the hole I was in.

After the side of the bed incident happened, I called the doctor and had him prescribe a different medication. Prozac was making me crazy. He called in Zoloft, which is another antidepressant and told me to call him after a week and let him know how it works.

Thank the Lord, after about five days the tremors and twitching stopped. I was finally able to at least function and get my bearings. I started eating a little more and would step outside onto my back deck and feel the sun on my face. I laid in bed for nearly a month.

With hesitation, I agreed to meet up with the band out in Washington for a show. I was nowhere near ready but Christy and the guys were wanting me to get back out there. I couldn't believe I had spent as much time as I did dealing with anxiety and depression. I wanted to at least try to get back to work.

I flew out of Nashville with my Bible in hand. I muddled through the airport like a zombie and boarded my flight. Once I settled into my seat the panic started. For the first time ever, I was scared to fly. For the next five hours I was a basket case. I prayed the whole way out there.

I knew I was flying into a tense situation. I would have to try to explain myself and justify why I took so much time to recover. I knew they'd be skeptical of my reasons for staying home. I had never been so fearful of a situation in all my life.

When I got there our new road manager, Jackie Williams, met up with me. He had been hired to fill Steve's role just a few months before I became sick. He was a good dude and really tried to accommodate me.

He was kind, but short with me. He got me checked into my room and let me know the schedule for the day. I was picked up by a person hired by the venue later that afternoon and headed to the gig.

Fear had gripped me like never before. I was so fidgety and didn't know how to tame it. I was having trouble breathing and my heart was racing a mile a minute. Inside my brain I scolded myself. How could I be such a pansy? How could I look at myself in the mirror from now on and not see a weak, pathetic man?

I remember stepping onto the stage for soundcheck. The guys just nodded and went about their business of setting up their gear. I played the show that night but I don't remember any of it. I was so crazy in my head that

I could hardly concentrate. Panic hit me three or four times during the set and I thought I'd have to exit the stage. I was seriously messed up and I honestly didn't know what to do.

When I finally got back to the hotel room, reality set in. I had to continue to be out there with people that didn't like me and I was mentally sick. I had to do something about it. What I did was out of desperation. I called our concession girl, Regina and I asked her if she'd give me a ride to the airport since she drove our concession truck.

I called my parents in Ohio and told them I was coming home. I had already booked a red eye flight from Washington to Cincinnati but not told any of the guys. I told my mom on the phone that I needed to see a psychologist. I was in a bad way.

Regina was kind enough to meet me in the lobby and take me to the airport. I boarded the plane knowing what the consequences of my decision might be. It was a big possibility that I'd be fired from the band. I worried myself to sleep that night on the plane and woke up at the Cincinnati airport.

The morning I got home I called Christy to tell him what had happened and why I needed to fly out. He was disappointed to say the least. I felt embarrassed for having to do what I did. But I knew I'd have been worthless out there if I had stayed.

For the next two weeks I stayed with Mom and Dad and saw a doctor in Cincinnati. I laid in bed and mostly just watched TV. My great aunt Tressie came to see me along with some of Mom's prayer warriors from church like Sister Setzer and Rosie Randazzo. They sat and prayed for me and told Satan to leave me alone. I sincerely felt like the Holy Spirit was with me and that God was bringing me out of the storm.

I had laid around for so long that my back was starting to hurt. I would try to get out of the house and walk around the block for some exercise. Dad would make me his famous turkey melts and Mom whipped up some of her peanut butter fudge.

Fairfield Ohio
From left to right: James Seals Jr., Jackie Seals and Brady Seals

The psychologist helped. It was his belief that my health condition was being caused by a chemical imbalance in my brain. It had something to do with my norepinephrine and serotonin levels.

I believe all these years later that he was right but that genes also have a hand in why depression strikes some people and not others. I know my mother struggled with it all of her life. I've read where as many as 40 percent of those with depression can trace it to a genetic link. Research has also shown that people with parents or siblings who have depression are up to three times more likely to have the condition.

The psychologist suggested that I needed to treat my brain just like a broken arm or leg. He said I needed time to heal and that with the proper rest and medication, I would eventually be alright. He felt the medicine I was taking was the proper medication for me, but it just needed a little more time to get into my system.

He also taught me breathing exercises when panic would hit me. He explained that the panic attacks would only last about twenty minutes each time and the rest of the time was just me worrying. I'd sit in his office with my eyes closed while he'd talk into a tape recorder. He'd talk about positive things like walking through an orange grove and smelling the citrus in the air. I could visualize myself being there and would start to calm down.

He sent me away with the recordings and told me to play them whenever I'd get panicky. For the most part it worked. For the next several weeks I could feel a difference in my mood. The combination of medicine, prayer and meditation was getting me back on my feet.

Looking back on it now I know without a shadow of doubt that the devil used depression and fear as a spiritual weapon against me and against God. The Bible describes that there's a spiritual war raging on this earth between the forces of good and evil. It has been going on since Satan was cast down from heaven.

"For we wrestle not against flesh and blood, but against principalities, against powers, against the rulers of the darkness of this world, against spiritual wickedness in high places." -Ephesians 6:12 KJV. It also says in Romans 7:22-23 NIV, *"For in my inner being I delight in God's law; but I see another law at work in me, waging war against the law of my mind and making me a prisoner of the law of sin at work within me."*

Clearly depression is an effective strategy that Satan is using. *"He will speak against the Most High and oppress his holy people and try to change the set times and the laws. The holy people will be delivered into his hands for a time, times and half a time." -Daniel 7:25 NIV*

When despair covers you up it can be really hard to dig your way out. But being proactive and talking to your doctor and staying in the Word of God, you can do it. Through Him all things all possible. *"Jesus said unto him, If thou canst believe, all things are possible to him that believeth." -Mark 9:23 KJV*

I knew I couldn't stay in Fairfield for the rest of my life, so I asked Mom and Dad to drive me back down to Bellevue. It was time to address the elephant in the room, Little Texas. I wanted to explain to the guys everything I had been through so they could see that I wasn't faking anything.

When I got back, Christy called and said that the band was nominated for an award for *Common Thread: The Songs of the Eagles*. It was up for the Country Music Associations, "Album of The Year". I wanted to attend the awards with the guys but was told they didn't want to sit by me.

I put in a call to Jim Ed Norman, the president of Warner Brothers to try to explain my situation. I wanted to give him my side of the story. I needed to tell him why I had not been on the road with the guys and that I wanted to be there at the awards ceremony.

Jim Ed was very sympathetic and let me know it'd be okay if I stayed home. He wished me well and hoped that I would get better soon. He also hoped that the guys would understand my predicament and welcome me back into the band with open arms.

After the conversation with Jim Ed, it inspired me to reunite with the guys. I called for a meeting at Christy's office on Music Row. I was nervous about it, so Dad rode down there with me. When I walked into Christy's office the whole band was there along with Christy and Doug Grau. Christy had set up the chairs in a circle for us to be able to see each other eye to eye. Initially everyone was very closed off. No one said anything when I walked in, except for Christy and Doug. I could tell the guys were infuriated that I took several months to recover.

I started first. I went through the timeline of when I first got sick. I told about the episode I had backstage of the Opry and the night Tiffany thought I was having a heart attack. I went through the list of doctors that I saw, the medications they prescribed, the side effects I experienced. I gave them the rundown of emotions I had felt, the desperation, the embarrassment and disappointment in myself.

I went on to describe the details of the days and nights to make them understand that I had reached the bottom and that I was determined to find my way back to the top. I let them know I stayed home because I had to, not because I wanted to. Tears rolled down while I told my story. I don't think I could've added anything more to my explanation. I had put it all out there.

When I finished, each one of the guys chimed in. One by one they told me how disappointed they were in me and how they had to carry the load for the last several months. One of them even said, "Someone told me they saw you out on your Harley, how sick can you be if you're riding your motorcycle?"

I tried to explain that I had always found peace in riding my bike, so I thought I might try riding it. I told him that I had to turn around and head back to the house after thirty minutes because I had another panic attack.

The look on his face told me he didn't believe me. Nothing I said was registering. They had already made up their minds about me. They believed that I was lying. I continued to plead my case and pretty much begged them to listen to me when the final blow came.

There I was with tears rolling down my face and feeling defeated when it got around to the last guy in the band's turn to talk. He looked at me with the most sincere face he could have and said, "I still think it's a bunch of bull s***."

It was like a dagger to the heart. I had had enough. I had just exposed my deepest emotions to the guys that I had grown to love as brothers and all I got was, "I still think it's a bunch of bull s***." I had gone months without hearing a word from them. I felt at that very moment they didn't care about me.

I looked around and said, "Well I guess we're done here then". I stood up and headed towards the door. I think Christy or Doug might've said, "Wait man" or "Hold on a second". The other guys didn't say anything. But I had reached my limit. I was not going to be treated like an outcast and misfit from a bunch of guys that had their own mental issues. Enough was enough.

My dad could see the anger in my eyes when I met him halfway in the parking lot. "What's wrong?" he said. "Do you want me to go in there and give 'em a piece of my mind?" I just said, "No Dad, just get in the truck. Let's go to the house."

That was it. I didn't see the guys again for two years. None of them tried to reach out to me and I didn't reach out to them. I hated leaving it unresolved. I felt sad that I wouldn't be hanging out with them anymore and playing music together. I felt bad for the fans too. They deserved better.

I felt the business had changed the dynamic of the band. Money had become the priority. But I also knew that we had formed bonds as people. We had become friends and to me that was what it was all about.

If the guys would've only been sympathetic and given me time to get well, I think everything would've been fine. I wanted to stay. But unfortunately, that's not the way it turned out.

For the next several months I just wandered around wondering what I was going to do. I had just quit a job making six figures a year. Now I had nothing. I knew that I would continue to receive royalty checks in the mail, but I didn't have a direction.

Thankfully, the prayers and medication were working and I began to think straight. I would occasionally have panic attacks but when that happened, I'd use my calming techniques to bring me back to normal. I used that time to get closer to God. I knew that even though it was hard, leaving the band was the right thing to do.

TOXICITY AND PAYING THE PIPER

I believe God uses relationships in our lives in instrumental ways. Some of the relationships are not healthy at all. They can happen between family members, friends, co-workers, bandmates and lovers. They teach us lessons and help us grow. They can mess with our happiness and self-esteem, they can make us feel depleted, and sometimes even hopeless. The Bible tells us, *"For where envying and strife is, there is confusion and every evil work." -James 3:16 KJV.* Toxic relationships bring negativity and strife to those who are in it.

2 Timothy 3-5 KJV says, *"This know also, that in the last days perilous times shall come. For men shall be lovers of their own selves, covetous, boasters, proud, blasphemers, disobedient to parents, unthankful, unholy, Without natural affection, trucebreakers, false accusers, incontinent, fierce, despisers of those that are good, Traitors, heady, highminded, lovers of pleasures more than lovers of God; Having a form of godliness, but denying the power thereof: from such turn away."*

Everyone deserves a second chance and people need grace when they make mistakes. We've all been the toxic one in the relationship at one point or the other, and by no means do I think we should just quit when times are hard. But if a friend, family or business relationship becomes unhealthy, it may be time to leave. The only exception would be marriage. God has different rules for that.

I also learned during this time of my life that sin will catch up with you. I finally had to pay the fiddler. *"But if ye will not do so, behold, ye have sinned against the LORD: and be sure your sin will find you out." -Numbers 32:23 KJV.* I had reached my capacity of holding onto all of the guilt. Those tremors that I had felt when hanging out with random girls in hotel rooms had manifested into something more severe and intense. It literally affected my nervous system.

I had to finally give it all to God. Once I did, my anxiety started to subside just like water after a storm. *"Do not be anxious about anything, but in every situation, by prayer and petition, with thanksgiving, present your requests to God. And the peace of God, which transcends all understanding, will guard your hearts and your minds in Christ Jesus." -Philippians 4:6-7 NIV*

CHAPTER SIX:
THE TRUTH

"O my God, incline thine ear, and hear; open thine eyes, and behold our desolations, and the city which is called by thy name: for we do not present our supplications before thee for our righteousnesses, but for thy great mercies." -Daniel 9:18 KJV

All in all, I laid around the house for six months before I was ready to socialize again. I stayed on my anti-depressant medicine for about nine months just to make sure I corrected whatever imbalance I had. I visited several churches during that time, but couldn't find the right fit. I had become used to Holiness churches and there were none to be had in Bellevue.

I remained vigilant in prayer and held onto Tiffany and we got closer and closer. I thanked God she was in my life. I felt the time was right to get back to playing and writing music. I wanted to feel like myself again. Maybe I could find another artist to play keyboards for or even embark on a solo project.

I called my cousin TJ, Troy's son to see if he might want to do some writing. TJ and I had reconnected a little and he knew all about my ordeal with Little Texas. He was sympathetic and a voice of reason for me during that time. I knew TJ was an extremely talented singer but I didn't know much about his writing skills.

I drove out to Hendersonville to where he lived. At the time he was still living with his parents. He had a killer music studio setup on the lower level of the house. It was filled with recording gear, guitars, keyboards and even an electronic drum kit. We fell right into a groove and away we went. I had been nervous that we wouldn't work well together since TJ was so pop and I was so country. But we did.

TJ's voice was a cross between Michael Jackson and Prince. Whenever we'd write, I let him sing. I just loved to hear how he interpreted the melody. Hearing what he did made me stretch out as a vocalist. The chord progressions we were experimenting with were a breath of fresh air. I realized that I had been using the same three or four chords for years.

After several months of writing and a few really great songs I was ready to start shopping them around. The first person I called was Jim Ed at Warner Bros. He was generous enough to take a meeting with me.

I had always respected Jim Ed. He was a tall, lanky man with a beaming smile. I had been told that he had a big connection to The Eagles. Evidently he had joined Don Henley's band back in the late '60s called Felicity. He later wrote the string arrangements for a bunch of The Eagles most iconic hits like "Desperado", "Hotel California" and "One of These Nights." While writing this chapter I found out that he's been asked to go out on the road with the Eagles to recreate those incredible arrangements on the Hotel California tour. Needless to say, the guy knew what he was doing.

It was the first time I had a one on one meeting with him in a room. The conversation was easy and loose. He had an effortless way of making me feel comfortable. During the talk he let me in on some of the details about the emotional dynamics and rocky personalities he had experienced with the Eagles. He clearly knew about the difficulties of life in a band.

I filled him in on the details of me leaving Little Texas and what I had been up to since then. I played him four or five songs. While he listened, I had a feeling that he wanted to sign me to the label. Afterwards, he told me he wanted me to keep writing and recording and to stay on the same musical path he had just heard.

I walked out of the office feeling hopeful. It had been awhile since I felt like everything was going to be okay. I was ready to get busy. When I got back home, I immediately called TJ and let him know that Jim Ed really dug what we were doing.

For the next several weeks I wrote like crazy. I also approached my buddies at CAA for ideas for management and to see if they were still interested in booking me. The CAA team was very receptive and they said yes, they did want to keep me on their roster. Rod Essig, one of the agents there also suggested I meet with a manager in Nashville named Burt Stein.

Burt worked at Gold Mountain Entertainment. GME also had an office in LA. I learned that Burt had worked as a promotions guy at a record label back in the seventies. When I met with him, he told me that he had worked with The Eagles, Linda Ronstadt, Jackson Browne and other influential artists that I loved.

Burt was a pleasure to be around as well. He had the kind of gentle spirit that I really needed at that time. I felt he and I could work well together and we signed a management contract not long after. I informed him that I had been managed by Christy and there might be some conflicts in the months to come. He didn't mind and said we'd figure it out as we moved forward.

Burt arranged a meeting with Rodney Crowell. Burt thought that he'd be a good record producer for me. Burt was managing Rodney at the time and was well aware that Rodney knew all the top musicians in town and could make truly great and unique records.

I already knew who Rodney was the day we met face to face over some chips and salsa. I remembered the *Diamonds and Dirt* record that he had released back in the late '80s and heard many of his songs, like "I Couldn't Leave You If I Tried", "She's Crazy For Leavin'" and "Above And Beyond", in every honky-tonk I had ever been in.

After chatting with him a few minutes, Rodney seemed like the perfect producer. He was very sympathetic with my emotional issues. We hit it off like long lost brothers. As for the direction to take with the album, he wanted me to just be myself. He also wanted me to stretch out a little as a singer and experiment with some new chord progressions. It was everything I wanted to hear.

The Nashville Network- Prime Time Country
From left to right: Brady Seals, Rodney Crowell and Gary
Chapman
Photo Credit: Tiffany Jones

It wasn't long before I was in the studio with him recording at Treasure Isle Recorders. It was one of Nashville's oldest independent studios. Dolly Parton, Johnny Cash, Isaac Hayes, Linda Ronstadt, Sheryl Crow and others had graced its space.

I had recorded there once before with Little Texas. Rodney brought in Peter Coleman to engineer the recordings. Peter had worked with a number of top-rated rock 'n roll and Americana artists like Blondie, The Knack, Kim Richie and Kevin Welch. I felt he could bring some rawness and honesty to the table, and I liked that. I absolutely did not want my record to sound like a typical Nashville album.

Rodney brought in all of the 'A' player musicians. Michael Rhodes, Tommy Harden, Paul Franklin, Steuart Smith and John Hobbs made up the studio band. These dudes were the best of the best. I had never been around guys that were so schooled at making records before. I was blown away by how quick they would lay down their tracks. I was in song heaven!

While searching for songs for the record, TJ had played me one that I knew was a hit. His dad (Troy) had written it with Will Jennings. It was called "Another You, Another Me." Rodney felt the same as me. We both knew that it was special. Rodney immediately thought that it would be a good duet song and called Wynonna Judd to see if she'd come in and sing on it with me.

I had long been a fan of The Judds. It was dream-like to be in the studio listening to Wynonna overdub her vocals on a song I was singing. She nailed it. I was thrilled to death to work with her.

I decided to name the album *The Truth* for several reasons. TJ and I had written a song called "The Truth," but I felt like the album was truly me. It also had a spiritual meaning, which I loved. The album and song were a little left of center in regards to a typical Nashville record. I loved that it had an edginess about it. The songs were well thought out and passionate. I was extremely proud of it.

TJ and I had written most of the songs with the help of TJ's friend Chris Bogan. I had also co-written another song with Tommy Barnes called "Still Standing Tall." And lastly Troy. I was so thankful to have his stamp on the record. I had always looked up to Troy and now here

I was writing songs with him and TJ. It was an amazing feeling to have it all come together like it did.

I was in a good place in my head. Occasionally the panic attacks would happen, but they weren't as demobilizing as they had been before. I was beginning to come out of the fog.

GOD'S GRACE AND MERCY

I can't proclaim it enough...our Father is full of grace and mercy. He restored my health AND gave me a new record deal. He didn't have to do either. I've often prayed for God's grace and mercy throughout my life but never really thought about the difference of the two words. Basically, God's grace and mercy can be described as two sides of the same coin. On one side, grace gives us what we do not deserve, and mercy on the other side does not give us what we do deserve.

The Greek for "grace", "charis" means either kindness, favor, "a gift or blessing brought to man by Jesus Christ", or "kindness which bestows upon one what he has not deserved" (Strong, James. 1890. *Strong's exhaustive concordance of the Bible.* Abingdon Press).

The Hebrew for "merciful" means "compassionate". It is derived from the root חסד châsad, Strong, James. 1890. *Strong's exhaustive concordance of the Bible.* Abingdon Press, which is usually translated as "to be merciful" or "to be kind." A related word what will help in understanding this meaning is the noun חסידה chăsîydâh (Strong, James. 1890. *Strong's exhaustive concordance of the Bible.* Abingdon

Press), meaning a "stork". The stork's curved neck provides a clue, which is the "bowing" of the head, which one would do when showing respect, kindness or mercy.

Ephesians 2 NIV explains God's grace and mercy best. *"As for you, you were dead in your transgressions and sins, in which you used to live when you followed the ways of this world and of the ruler of the kingdom of the air, the spirit who is now at work in those who are disobedient. All of us also lived among them at one time, gratifying the cravings of our flesh and following its desires and thoughts. Like the rest, we were by nature deserving of wrath. But because of his great love for us, God, who is rich in mercy, made us alive with Christ even when we were dead in transgressions—it is by grace you have been saved. And God raised us up with Christ and seated us with him in the heavenly realms in Christ Jesus, in order that in the coming ages he might show the incomparable riches of his grace, expressed in his kindness to us in Christ Jesus. For it is by grace you have been saved, through faith—and this is not from yourselves, it is the gift of God— not by works, so that no one can boast. For we are God's handiwork, created in Christ Jesus to do good works, which God prepared in advance for us to do."*

God continually gives us grace and mercy every time we breathe and every step we take once we become a believer. He has saved us from eternal condemnation and the incredible gift of never-ending life with Him and His Son Jesus. Hallelujah!

Chapter Seven:
Heavenly View

"Thine, O Lord is the greatness, and the power, and the glory, and the victory, and the majesty: for all that is in the heaven and in the earth is thine; thine is the kingdom, O Lord, and thou art exalted as head above all." -1st Chronicles 29:11 KJV

When all of the recording was done Burt and I decided to have a showcase for the label and for the booking agency. We invited all of the people involved with the record and those we felt would help us get the first single on the radio. We set up our gear at a rehearsal facility in Nashville called SIR. I hired a lighting company to come out and we installed a top-notch lighting rig. I wanted to make sure the booking agents could imagine my live show in amphitheaters and large stages.

We rocked that night. I gave it my all. I remember Burt coming up to me and saying that after the show, Jim Ed told him, "It was one of the best showcases I've ever seen...but what do I do with it?" Burt and I were confused by his comment. It seemed Jim Ed thought the songs were not as commercial as he wanted them to be and felt like it might be hard to get them played on the radio. Deep down it made me angry. I felt I had made a record that was innovative but yet still very viable for radio.

Burt and I were bewildered but we kept moving forward and hoping for the best. We believed that the songs would speak for themselves and radio would get onboard once the record was released. I spent the next three or four months on a radio promotion tour, visiting all the prominent stations and talking up the new single. I also picked Gerry Wenner to direct the video for the first single since I had had so much luck with him in the past.

"Another You, Another Me" was released on September 7th, 1998 to radio and CMT. It came out of the chute like a bucking pony. Radio stations all over America played it and people all over the world bought it. The ballad sold over 100,000 copies. That was a big number back then. We all thought we had something special on our hands. It was described by Wendy Newcomer of *Cash Box* magazine as having a sound similar to England Dan and John Ford Coley.

Brady Seals
Photo Credit: Sherry Arnold and Niki Lee

CAA also had me out doing show after show and everything seemed to be working perfectly. I had picked up right where I left off from Little Texas except this time, I was my own boss. I called all the shots. I hired a killer band and called them The Natural Born Lovers. I even hired Lua Crofts, Dash Crofts' daughter, to be in the group. It was pretty cool to have a new generation of Seals & Crofts on stage again.

With the song halfway up the charts, I felt Warner Bros. pull back the reins. I was constantly calling Burt to ask what was going on. He didn't understand what was happening either. The single had all the right elements. Rodney Crowell produced it, Troy and Will wrote it, Wynonna was singing background, I had just come off of a number one single with "My Love," and the public loved it.

Something happened though and to this day I'm still not quite sure what. I do know that Warner Bros. totally missed the boat on record sales for the album. They didn't release it until five months after the single. I remember being livid each time we'd ask when the CD was coming out and they put it off and put it off. I continued to do my job on the road though.

I had been asked to fly out to Vegas and sing the song for five couples that got married at the same time. The song had really connected to those that actually heard it on the radio. I had people coming up to me all the time saying that it was the song they danced to at their wedding. Some schools even used it for their high school graduation song.

I got word that Trisha Walker, an international booking agent booked a European tour for me. It had been several years since I had crossed The Atlantic and I wanted to get back over there and establish myself as an artist. I loved traveling to new places and seeing how other cultures lived.

Our first big show was in Mragowo, Poland. It was a huge outdoor event called The Piknik Country & Folk festival. We stayed there for three days. Concert goers came from miles around and pitched tents around the Great Masurian Lakes. Each night you could walk from camp to camp hearing people laughing and singing by their own fires. It was kinda like Poland's country version of Woodstock.

The day before the show Trisha had arranged for me and the band to counsel and teach some music enthusiasts at a school house. We each had interpreters in our rooms so the students could understand us. We taught about music theory, the history of country music and show business. Initially I was a little nervous about doing it but it turned out to be a wonderful experience.

The show itself was sensational and the crowd seemed to absolutely love the music. We were all stunned at how wild the audience was. We had to come back with two encores. We made a lot of friends during those three days and I told Trisha, "We have to come back."

The next stop was Switzerland for several shows. One in Gstaad and the other in Interlaken. It was magical. I just fell in love with the views of the mountains. I remember us taking an aerial cableway up the mountain and visiting Restaurant Piz Gloria. It sets at an altitude of 2970 meters and with floor-to-ceiling windows. The restaurant rotates around its own axis every forty-five minutes so guests can get 360-degree views of the mountains. It's the same place that in 1969, the year I was born, that the James Bond film "On Her Majesty's Secret Service" was shot.

I recall having to do an interview with a radio station in England while dining up there. I truly felt like I was on top of the world. The view was heavenly. I remember having a silent conversation with God and thanking Him for what He had done for me and bringing me to that place. For a moment everything made sense and I was so incredibly content. God had answered my prayers.

I also experienced another heavenly view when I got back down in the town of Interlaken. I remember standing there with Greg McDowell, who was now playing guitar in my band, and seeing something special. We had finished dinner and played an acoustic show for a promoter when Greg and I stepped out to clear our heads. We walked down by a crystal-clear river that was running right through town and overlooking the Alps, when all of a sudden, a large white Mute Swan came floating by us. We were both spellbound. We looked at one another and said, "Well, that'll never happen again" and then seconds later, there came another one.

Switzerland was hard to leave. I had fallen in love with the landscape, the food and the people, but we had to continue on with the tour. We also played an outdoor concert in Craponne, France. I remember having a panic attack before the show and had to lie down in a little travel trailer. I still wasn't over my anxiety and had daily occurrences while overseas.

I was able to get through the show though. The audience had no idea I was freaking out on the inside.

After the gig, the mayor of Craponne presented me with a small golden token on behalf of the city which made me feel like royalty. Once again, the townspeople were so engaging and appreciative. It was cool to know there were country music fans everywhere, even in France.

Brady Seals in front of the Eiffel Tower
Paris, France

The Natural Born Lovers
From left to right: Mark "Billfold" Ford, Mark "Sparky" Matejka, Andy, Todd, Brady Seals, Bob McDowell, Greg McDowell, Ty Smith, Paul Chapman and Steve Emily

When we arrived back in the states it was business as usual. I got right back into writing and doing more shows. The single started to fizzle out on the charts and we knew it was time to plan for the next release. I was frustrated at the lack of commitment from Warner Bros. It appeared that they had given up on the single.

The next two single releases fared even worse. We released the songs, "Still Standing Tall" and "Natural Born Lovers." Neither one of them broke the top fifty on the charts. The releases were complete failures. We had lost all momentum from the initial single release and never recovered. I tried everything in my power to promote them as well. I probably did more free shows for radio stations in 1997 than I ever had before.

I kept going though. I tried to mark it up as what the label kept saying. "To radio, you're just a new artist" or "you have to establish yourself as a viable act first." I had to trust the label no matter how I felt. I was told by Burt and Rodney to just give them what they wanted on the next record. I figured Rodney would know best since he'd been an artist before, and he was highly regarded in Nashville.

So that's just what I did. I started writing and recording very commercial songs. I didn't want my opinion to get in the way this time. I got together with Tommy Barnes and we really tried to find a hit single. One day he played me one that I had heard years before and loved. It was called "I Fell". I thought it sounded like a hit and when I played it for Rodney, he was onboard too.

There was only one hold up. Tommy was good friends with Tim McGraw and he had a song deal with Tim. The deal was that Tim had first dibs on any song that Tommy wrote. That made me nervous because I knew there was a big possibility that Tim would cut the song first.

I remember the day when I was sitting in the bleachers with Tommy and Tim discussing the song. We were all just hanging out before one of Tim's shows at the arena in Nashville. Tim loved the song but chose to pass on it. I'm not sure his exact reason but it didn't matter to me. I loved it. I didn't show my excitement in front of him but inside I was ecstatic about his decision.

For the next several months I was in writing mode and obsessed with finding hit singles. In the meantime, Rodney had negotiated a new deal with Warner Bros. for me. When I released *The Truth*, I was signed to Reprise Records, which was a label affiliated with Warner Bros. Now they wanted me on the main label. We were able to ask for a new record budget.

Rodney and I decided to record at Ocean Way Recording this time. A lot of successful records were being made there and we wanted to make sure our tracks sounded similar. They had a large SSL mixing console there and everyone raved about how good it sounded. We recorded the tracks with most of the same guys from the first record along with a few new incredible musicians.

We recorded most of the vocals at my house in Bellevue. I had bought a Fred Cameron modified Neumann U87 microphone. Fred was known around town for his expertise for taking a normal U87 mic and making it tube. Fred would make little custom boxes for the mics that were essentially a preamp with a tube in it. It warmed up the sound so much and I loved how it made my voice sound. After asking Peter Coleman to help me find the right vocal sound for me he suggested a few options. I settled on a vintage Telefunken V76 and a black faced vintage Urei 1176 for my signal chain.

The Telefunken and the Urei are considered outboard gear in the recording studio. The units fit in a studio rack where a microphone or any audio signal like a guitar, bass or keyboard plugs into it. My microphone would plug into the Telefunken preamp first and then into the Urei compressor. The output of the Urei would travel to the audio interface to be recorded.

I remember one day Rodney had some incredible singers come over to the house and lay down their background vocals. It was Vince Gill, Timothy B. Schmit (from the Eagles), Chris Rodriguez and Max Carl of .38 Special. There were several times I had to pinch myself to make sure I wasn't in a dream. These dudes could sing!

The Purple Room, Bellevue Tennessee
From left to right: Chris Rodriguez, Brady Seals, Timothy B. Schmit, Max Carl, Rodney Crowell and Herb Tassin
Photo Credit: Tiffany Jones

Rodney also called some other friends that made appearances on the record like Bela Fleck, Jerry Douglas, John Cowen, Paul Liem and Ricky Skaggs. I had no doubt that the record would sound incredible. We pulled out all the stops to make a memorable album.

We released "I Fell" in 1998 along with a video. We seriously thought this was the one. We had planned and plotted to make sure we crossed all the "T"s and dotted all the "I"s. I got out on the road to play shows immediately to support the single. I was flying to radio stations every chance I could get to let them know about my new release. I had a smokin' band and I was ready for what the label threw at me. I was feeling so much better inside too. The anxiety had calmed, the panic subsided and I was finally feeling healthy.

The problem was that when I would show up at some of the radio stations the program directors would tell me that the label hadn't contacted them to let them know that my single was available to play. Time after time I'd get the same story. One program director up in the Northeastern region said that Warner Bros. wasn't playing the same game as the rest of the labels.

Of course, I was puzzled and disappointed. Burt and I didn't know what to do. We had a well thought out CD, but the record label wasn't behind it. I had put everything on the line for this one. The radio stations that were playing the song said it was performing well. I didn't understand what was happening.

The next thing I did was not like me at all, but I felt it needed to be done. I made a list of all of the comments from the radio stations I had visited and jotted down all the other issues that were happening with the label, and called for a meeting with the head of promotion at Warner.

I had filled two pages worth of complaints about how the label was dropping the ball. I tried to be as direct as I could, without being a jerk. I put it all on the line because I knew that I had come too far to let my sophomore record fail. The promotion guy just sat there and tried to explain why the singles were failing. Nothing made sense to me. I felt in my soul that after that meeting the rest of the singles were also going to fall flat.

And that's exactly what happened. "I Fell" peaked at 55 on the Billboard Chart. The next single "Whole Lotta Hurt," struggled to get to 66 and "The Best Is Yet To Come," stalled at number 74. I couldn't believe that the label had all of the goods to have a hit record but just couldn't make it happen. I was so disheartened with them and their way of doing things. My career had taken a dive because of the label's refusal to make it happen.

After getting Burt's approval, I finally had a sit-down meeting with the general manager, Bob Saporiti, and Jim Ed at a little Mexican restaurant and told them I would be leaving the label when my contract was up. I appreciated Jim Ed signing me, but I couldn't let this go on anymore. They did not attempt to keep me on their label as an artist, and appeared to have no regrets at all. I knew then that I made the right call.

Once I was finally free of my stint with Warner Bros. I needed a breather from major labels. I had been beat up from the feet up. I didn't feel relevant at all. I felt I wouldn't be missed at all from the Music Row machine. I felt like I had been chewed up and spat out. I figured that I needed to step away from the business for a while.

Tiffany and I had reached the end of our road as well. We had tried for years to make it work. I loved her no doubt. I had even asked her to marry me after one of our arguments. I really wanted to make it work with her but over and over we just couldn't get along. Regretfully I had to call off the engagement after three months because of our bickering. I was heartbroken and so was she. We both loved one another but, in the end, we had to go our separate ways.

Several positive things came out of that period of my life though. One was the farm. I had seen the listing in a home magazine at a Kroger supermarket while getting groceries one day. It was a log home from 1865 on 140 acres on sale for $187,000. I couldn't believe my eyes at first. I called Burt who had a vintage Triumph motorcycle and asked him if he'd like to ride out to the place and take a look at it. We rode one and a half hours west to Erin, Tennessee.

When we rolled up on the joint, I was in shock. The place was straight out of a dream. I walked the grounds a little and looked inside the little cabin. I fell in love with it. I could imagine coming out there and just chillin' on days off, getting away from the ruckus of city life. I had to have it and I had the money to do it.

Even though I had my house in Bellevue, two Corvettes (a 1966 split-window and a 1963 convertible), a Chevy truck and a Harley; I still had enough in the bank to put a down payment on it. I called the real estate agent right away and asked to see the inside and view the plot. All it took was seeing the inside of what looked to be like the home of The Ingalls on the TV show, *Little House on The Prairie* and I was sold. I made an offer immediately.

I settled close to the asking price and closed on it within a month of seeing it. The guy that owned it was named McDonald, so essentially, I bought old McDonald's farm. I also found out that part of the home used to be the old Erin post office. Incredibly, the place came with two big barns, an old Ford tractor, a farm truck and a dirt bike.

That year I threw a huge Halloween party and invited all my friends from Nashville. Mom and Dad came down from Ohio and helped me with getting it ready along with some other friends, The Hubka's. It was quite a drive for them but once they got there, they realized why I bought it. We partied through the night and I had an enormous bonfire. I'm sure all the locals wondered who the heck had just moved into their neighborhood!

I also got a little border collie puppy after purchasing the farm. I figured I needed a good farm dog. I named her Gypsy. She was black and white and smart as could be. She was also full of energy and loved running through the open fields.

Mom didn't know what to think of the place because she had been a city girl most of her life. Dad on the other hand loved it. Whenever he'd come down, he'd spend all day outside fiddling around doing this and that. He'd work from sun up to sun down without stopping. I'm so thankful I got to spend those moments with them. I wouldn't trade it for the world.

The other positive opportunity was getting to write and record with Andy Sturmer. I had been a huge fan of his music after I heard his band Jellyfish on the bus one evening while out with Little Texas. We had been given two or three boxes of free CDs from the record label. The boxes were filled with all kinds of music from Warner Bros. and other subsidiary labels they were involved with.

Rusty told me to check out one of the CDs because he thought I'd dig it, and dig it, I did. When I first listened to *Bellybutton*, Jellyfish's first CD, I was bewildered. The vocals and production of the songs were on a whole other level. Their music was a cross between Queen, The Beach Boys, The Beatles and Badfinger.

I couldn't stop listening. I was able to track down their second album, *Split Milk* and I freaked out. I was like a kid in a candy store. I felt I had found a diamond in a pile of rocks. I was so tired of the same old sounds and the same old hooks and phrases. Jellyfish broke the mold.

I found out everything I could about them. They were based out of San Francisco, California. They recorded both of their albums with producer Albhy Galuten and engineer Jack Joseph Puig and had been touring with The Black Crowes.

I read in the liner notes that Andy was not only the drummer and lead singer but one of the main songwriters for the band. I did some more research and found out who Andy's management company was and called them. I knew that it was a long shot, but I really wanted to write with him. I wanted to see if we could find some common ground between his style of music and mine. I told the assistant who I was and that I'd love to have the opportunity to get together with Andy and create some music.

Several weeks later Andy called. I couldn't believe it. I was a little giddy on the phone since I was such a fan, but I kept it together enough to have a good conversation. He was intrigued by the idea of mixing pop and country. We struck up a friendship that would later change the way I wrote and recorded.

I had arranged for him to come to Nashville and stay at the house for several days and we wrote constantly. His knowledge and musical sense were unlike any person I had ever written with. His melodies were so innovative.

Andy was heavily influenced by The Beatles and you could tell it in his chord structures. He was primarily a drummer but his guitar skills were spot on too. I'm not sure what he saw in me. I would just sit there most of the time, starry eyed and listening to him sing and play all of his intricate melodies.

I guess he did see something in me though. We arranged another trip where I'd come out to his place in Sea Ranch, California to write. I stayed for about a week and it was life changing. I had just said goodbye to Warner Bros., my anxiety had calmed way down, and I was ready for a new direction.

Andy was like a human music history book. Whenever we'd start writing a song, he'd compare the melody to an iconic artist from the past and then go listen to those old songs. He'd hear little chord changes or signature licks and revamp them for the song we were writing. I had never used that technique before but it worked like a charm. We never seemed to get in a rut. We were constantly drawing inspiration from artists that came before us.

The other skill I learned was working in Pro Tools, a digital audio workstation designed for music creation and production. I had used the software program before with Herb Tassin editing the sequence of a record, but not to record individual tracks. I had been using Alesis ADATS and other digital multitrack recorders like Otari Radar to lay down my tracks. With Pro Tools, you could actually see the audio waveforms on the computer screen and edit it visually.

After experiencing how Andy recorded, I traded in my rig and bought the latest and greatest Pro Tools software and interface. There was definitely a learning curve but after months and months of pushing record and play, it started to make sense. Instead of mixing everything down to a two track and storing it on a DAT tape and sending that by mail to Andy, I was now mixing it down to a file that I could send via the Internet.

The Internet blew my mind. More and more people were using it to communicate. The buzz at the time was America Online. People were starting to chat around the globe online in real time. We were also starting to use email to send documents back and forth. It made it a lot easier to get things done.

Even though long-distance communication had gotten better overall, it was still hard to get Andy on the phone and finish some of the projects we had going. I finally asked him if he was okay with me finishing the record without him. I didn't want to, but I really needed to finish. The clock was ticking and I knew that if I didn't turn in something soon, my window of opportunity would close.

TESTS INTO TESTIMONIES

Seems like life is one big roller coaster doesn't it? One day you're up, one day you're down. One day you're on a mountaintop and the next you're down in a valley. Know that you're not alone. Every biblical character in The Bible went through these "ups and downs" as well.

* There was Job who was wealthy and healthy and on top of the world. Within a few verses, he's down in the dumps, sores covered his body, he was in mourning from losing his family and was poverty stricken.
* John the Baptist became the most renowned preacher in four centuries. But just like that...he's in prison.
* David went on to describe in Psalms how God lifted him up from the bottom. He went from weeping to joy, from poverty to prosperity, from mourning to dancing and from silence to singing.

It happens to us all in today's world as well. Life isn't ideal and we will go through trials and tribulations. But hopefully we can turn our tests into testimonies, our mess into a message. Our stories can help fellow brothers and sisters through their struggles. We can spread the good news about how our God is faithful and how He carried us through it all.

Whether we are up or down, He remains steadfast, our Rock. *"He is the Rock, his work is perfect: for all his ways are judgment: a God of truth and without iniquity, just and right is he." -Deuteronomy 32:4 KJV*

CHAPTER EIGHT:
CEDAR LANE

*"The bricks are fallen down, but we will build with hewn stones:
the sycamores are cut down, but we will change them into cedars."*
-Isaiah 9:10 KJV

I didn't keep up with my old band mates, Little Texas. I had heard a couple of their singles, "Life Goes On" and "Bad For Us," but that's about it. I was still very hurt by what happened and evidently, they were too. My old friend Jeff Huskins went on to replace me in the band. They lasted another four years without me before they broke up.

I never wished them ill will. I figured that if they kept doing what they were doing on the road it would keep the songs fresh and the royalties on the songs I wrote would keep coming. I was thankful to them for that.

When I left the band, I didn't ask for a dime. I figured since I was the one who left, it wasn't fair for me to ask them to keep paying me royalties on the band name, so I just signed over my rights. I guess some might think that was stupid of me since I was part of the original lineup, but I just didn't feel it was right for me to walk away and still want something from them. I have no regrets.

For the next several years I enjoyed time on the farm and spent hours on my four-wheeler. I'd go out on the weekends and listen to the crickets and watch the clouds roll by. I made some new friends that lived down the road and enjoyed the simple life. I'd get on my tractor and bush hog the fields, camp out under the stars and I even went coon hunting one night with the locals. I loved being able to just relax for a little while and not have to be anywhere.

One night stands out in my mind about those times on the farm. I had invited David and Jared, two childhood friends from Ohio, to spend the weekend at the cabin. I figured it'd be fun to get together and reminisce a little.

We all rode four wheelers and I introduced them to my new friend Donnie who lived down the road. We hung out and I showed them the campsite I had cleared out in the woods. I had some hammocks hanging up next to a fire pit that was surrounded by stones. It was a perfect spot, right next to a beautiful running creek.

Each of us found a hammock to lay in and we started telling funny childhood stories. I had an old Coleman lantern that I hung on a tree branch to give us a little more light than the fire could provide. It was so much fun that we decided we'd crash there for the night. The temperature was perfect. We all just laid there zoned out looking up at the trees and sky.

I remember rambling on about something when all of a sudden, I heard a whizzing noise followed by a small thump. I stopped in mid-sentence and said, "Did y'all hear that?" And sure enough they heard it too. We all laid there for a second, but didn't hear anything else.

I went right back into my ramble when I heard it again. "Zzzzzzzz….fump!" I sat up immediately and started to look around the campsite. I thought for a second that maybe there was someone in the woods shooting BBs at us. I looked over at the lantern and I saw, what I thought was a moth, when suddenly I saw another moth come flying in at a hundred miles per hour and it hit the lantern straight on. It hit it so hard that the lantern moved!

Everyone was up at this point. That's when I heard something fly by my head and I could hear the wings moving. It went straight for the lantern. About that time Donnie yelled out, "I think it's hornets!" We all freaked. I knew we needed to get out of there fast. We frantically got our things together when we saw more and more of those little kamikazes. At this point they're buzzin' all around the camp, attracted by the fire.

We ran over to the four wheelers and sped off to the cabin in a panic. Once we went inside, we died laughing. We were truly thankful that we escaped with our lives. But the more I sat there, the more I started to realize that those hornets ruined our perfect campsite. We started scheming about how we could battle the hornets.

Donnie called his Dad and he said the only way to get rid of them was to burn 'em out. He said we'd have to get a big long stick with some material wrapped around the end of it and douse it with Kerosene and light it on fire and then stick in the hornet's nest. Looking back on it, I don't think he actually thought we'd be stupid enough to try it.

But we were. We rigged up a hornet killing device to go head to head with the hornets. Donnie got in his truck and I got in mine. Jared and David rode with me. We drove up to the campsite from the side where there was a big hay field so we could shine the truck lights on the mission zone.

We got out and lit that material on fire. Donnie was brave enough to hold the stick and I told him I'd be right by his side shining the flashlight so he could see where to go. We slowly walked closer and closer. Luckily, I spotted the hornet's nest immediately. Jared and David walked behind us giggling and rooting us on.

We knew we had to go in quick, poke that nest with the stick, leverage it into the ground so it'd stay, and then run. And that's just what we did. I remember us running like scared rabbits.

When we finally got back into the trucks, we could see the hornets hitting the windshield. Adrenaline rushed through our veins and we all were breathing heavily, as if we had just run 100 yards for a touchdown. We laughed 'til we cried. We then wheeled the trucks around and headed back to the cabin to get some sleep.

I bought the farm thinking I could go out there and just relax but after three years, it had become a lot of work as well. Every time I would visit, I'd have to get busy fixing something like the sub-pump or replace the rotten wood on the fence. It was non-stop. The time had come in my life to totally downsize.

I had found a home that I really liked in Hillsboro Village in Nashville and decided that it was time to sell my home in Bellevue. I realized that if I moved from

Bellevue to Nashville, my drive to the farm would take two hours. I certainly didn't want to have to do that every time I wanted to get away, so I decided to sell the farm as well.

I sold all kinds of stuff during the move. I got rid of both of my Corvettes, the tractor, the dirt bike and both my trucks. It was time to lighten my load and do away with a bunch of stuff that I was having to maintain.

Before I knew it, the farm and the Bellevue house sold and the owner of the new house on Cedar Lane accepted my offer. I moved in and immediately started renovating the place. My friend Mike Hubka, my dad and I set in to spiff up the 1939 cottage. Mike was a handyman and was experienced with plumbing and carpentry. Dad had worked as a foreman for a construction company after he retired from Fisher Body and I had a little experience too. My first job, when I was 15, was framing for a construction company. I took the next six months to fix up the house and finish up my CD.

I learned so much during that time, thanks to Mike. We ripped out walls, ran plumbing, built walls, laid tile, put up drywall and painted. All the while I lived downstairs in the dust. Looking back now I'm not really sure why I chose to put myself through such changes. I guess I just wanted to prove to myself that I could do something other than play music.

I enjoyed the renovation process. It was therapeutic for me in a way. I really had a passion for houses. I loved the architectural aspect of it. I loved it so much that I entertained the thought of flipping houses for a living instead of being a recording artist.

I had fallen in love with the process of shopping for real estate and my friend Richard Courtney who worked for Village Real Estate in Nashville said I'd be a good Realtor. I hadn't considered any other profession since I was 16 years old but I thought, "Why not?" Richard advised me where to go for my schooling to get my license and I enrolled. For about a year I dabbled in it but eventually decided not to move forward with it as a career. There was just too much financial risk in it.

I was going through so many changes during that time and I was trying desperately to find my direction. It seemed like the new house being renovated was much like my life. I felt like God was teaching and showing me things and I had been in dire need of repair. It took Him a little while to fix but eventually it got done.

All the while I was hammering and improving, I started laying the foundation for the record. Andy and I had written a song or two that set the tone and direction. My cousin TJ added his touch to the record along with a few other co-writer friends. TJ had started a song called "Thompson Street" that I thought was perfect for the CD. It had this 1980s, Rolling Stones thing about it that I loved. I decided to make it the title track.

I brought in Steuart Smith to play guitar on it. I remember the day well. I saw him pull up in the driveway and he sat in his car, talking on the phone for a while before coming into the house. I hadn't seen him since he played on my last solo record so it was good to catch up with him when he finally did make his way inside.

He came into the door and sat his guitars down, but he looked dazed and confused. I was like, "Hey man!...how have you been brother?" He replied, "Man, I've been great but I'm a little baffled right now and I don't know what to do?". I said, "What do you mean man?" He went on to say, "Well, Shawn Colvin wanted me to go out on the road with her and I promised Rodney Crowell I'd do some of his live shows, but I just got off the phone with Don Henley." I anxiously stood there to see where the conversation was going. He continued, "I'm just not sure what to do or who to go out with. Don wants me to go out on the road with The Eagles."

I laughed and said, "Cry me a river!...that's quite a dilemma." I explained, "You gotta go out with The Eagles, it'll open up so many doors for you brother." He finished by saying, "Yeah, I know it's a great opportunity, I just don't know how I feel about playing Felder's parts all the time and not being able to be creative." I told him, "Man, it's something you have to do. This gig will open up a whole new world for you. Before too long they'll see how freakin' talented you are and want to use you in the studio if they start making new music."

Well sure enough Steuart went on to become a member of The Eagles. I know he felt bad about not being able to deliver for Shawn and Rodney, but I'm sure they understood and probably congratulated him on the new milestone gig.

While I was tracking one day I went out for some lunch and dropped into a place located in Hillsboro Village called The Trace. I was moseying around looking for a waitress to order something to go when I saw Lisa Stewart sitting there with a friend of hers. It had been a year or so since I had seen her at her birthday party, but I recognized her immediately.

I asked her how she'd been and we had some small talk. Both of us had moved on from our past relationships and I thought she was very engaging and pretty. I asked for her telephone number, but she gave me her email address instead.

The next day I was so excited to contact Lisa, I went over to a friend 's house that had Internet and I sent her a message. I would've sent it from home but my house was still in shambles and I hadn't hooked up my service yet. She got back in touch with me within the next day or two and we set up our first date.

I remember sitting with her over dinner and feeling very comfortable. We mostly talked about the music business and our love lives. Lisa had grown up in Mississippi, in a small town called Louisville. Her mother and father had supported her through the years as a singer and she seemed to have the same kind of principles as me. She was also a Christian and had the identical political views as I did. She was also beautiful and so easy to talk to, we got along great. I was pleasantly surprised at how much we had in common. I knew I wanted to see her again after only an hour of being around her.

I would've asked to see her the next evening but she was supposed to go down to Mississippi to see her family. I had to settle for just talking on the phone with her instead. She had told me she'd give me a call when she got on the road so we could talk. I remember pacing around the house waiting for her to call.

When I finally did talk to her, I was absolutely stunned about what she said. Evidently, she had a guy friend that had told her this crazy story about me that got her all upset and made her very reluctant to ever see me again.

The story was that I had been in a relationship with Tanya Tucker and I had two children living in Florida. The tale took a turn for the worse when I had supposedly beaten Tanya, and that's the reason we broke up.

When she asked me if it was true, I laughed...hard! It was the most ridiculous thing I had ever heard. I told her that whoever told her that story was misinformed and I had no idea where that craziness came from. Lisa seemed to believe me but I'm sure she was still skeptical.

She'd been in the music business for quite some time and would've heard about me being in an abusive relationship like that. To this day I don't know how that lie was generated. I think her friend was just trying to throw a wrench in Lisa's new plans because he liked her more than a friend.

Luckily, Lisa believed me, and we continued to see each other. I found out through talking with her that her condo was only four or five blocks from me. We decided that we'd take an evening stroll and meet in the middle at a bridge overlooking the 440 Interstate. The more I saw her, the more I wanted to see her.

Thank God the renovations were coming to an end. I was tired of breathing dust and smelling paint fumes. The whole upstairs had been renovated. It felt great to have accomplished such a task.

I remember clearly one particular morning when she was over at my house. I was upstairs getting ready while she was downstairs and she yelled for me to come down quickly. I was concerned that maybe she had hurt herself. When I came into the living room, I saw it. She was watching the news and one of the twin towers in New York was on fire. We both spent the rest of the day witnessing the horror of the terrorist attacks on September 11, 2001.

It was sobering to say the least. We felt frightened, sad and angry at the same time. I wanted to either move to Australia and get away from all of it or join the armed forces and fight against the people who had done that. I couldn't believe what I saw. For the next week or so it was all anyone talked about.

The whole episode made me stop and re-examine my time on earth. It made me realize how short life was and what was truly important. I wanted to spend more time with my family and possibly start a new one with Lisa.

I spent the next year finishing up the CD. I had really hoped that Andy and I would've been able to finish it together, but it just didn't happen that way. I had enjoyed every second of collaborating with him and learned a great deal during the process.

Experimenting on *Thompson Street* made me grow as an artist and even though it didn't turn out exactly how I had imagined, it needed to happen. I had my friend Peter Coleman mix it and prepare the tracks for pressing.

I went to Burt with the project and thankfully he found a company called Image Entertainment to distribute the record for me. It was a way for me to release it independently and still get my CDs in retail stores.

We didn't really release anything to radio and I didn't feel like touring. I just didn't want to go through the process of putting together a band, and truthfully, I didn't feel any of the songs fit a particular genre of radio. I knew that the CD wouldn't really connect to most of my fan base either. Most of them were country music lovers. I made the record for me.

After releasing *Thompson Street* in 2003, I needed a break. My heart and soul were tired. I felt lost musically, and I needed some time to recuperate. I wanted to focus on my new relationship with Lisa and not put so much emphasis on my career. I had been going non-stop for about fifteen years and wanted to take the needle off the record for a while.

Burt had been a true gentleman as a manager and he endured a lot of drama during our contract together. When I finally told him I'd like to take some time off, he understood. We finished up some live show dates on the calendar and shut the operation down.

I also had a wonderful business manager at the time, Gary Haber. His general manager, Dawn Nepp and his staff at Haber Corporation helped me tie up all the financial loose ends. It was kind of a bittersweet thing for me to pause my career, but it had to be done.

He Maketh Me Lie Down

The one big lesson I learned after leaving Little Texas was to never overload my mind and body again. It causes anxiety which can lead to depression. God doesn't want us to be worried and full of fear. Isaiah 41:10 KJV says, *"Fear thou not; for I am with thee: be not dismayed; for I am thy God: I will strengthen thee; yea, I will help thee; yea, I will uphold thee with the right hand of my righteousness."* We also need to rest sometimes. It's crucial for our health. God showed us by example even He pauses. He rested on the seventh day after creation. -Genesis 2:2.

There have been so many times in my life where God showed me that it was time to slow down. In Psalm 23:2 KJV says, *"He maketh me to lie down in green pastures: He leadeth me beside the still waters."* He doesn't lead us in pastures for our sake, it's all for His sake, His glory. We can only benefit from it because of His grace.

Notice what Psalm 23:3 KJV says…*"He restoreth my soul: he leadeth me in the paths of righteousness for his name's sake."* It's His desire to restore us and to revitalize us. He wants us to be healthy and happy. He is The Prince of Peace. -Isaiah 9:6

If you're like me…a workaholic, it's hard to slow down. But you have to take God's advice and know when to put on the brakes. Take time to enjoy God's creation, appreciate what God has given you, spend time with your family and friends and soak up God's blessing of life. He knows what you need and He'll guide you there. All you need to do is trust in Him. Lay in the green pastures and sit beside the still waters for a while.

CHAPTER NINE:
CHAMELEON

"Therefore shall a man leave his father and his mother, and shall cleave unto his wife: and they shall be one flesh."
-Genesis 2:24 KJV

Lisa and I were inseparable. Most nights we'd stay up late listening to music and figuring out the world's problems. The more I spent time with her, the more I realized how bright she was. She had spent three years at Belmont University before becoming a country music artist. She had great drive and tenacity. I began to notice in our conversations that I would continually get lost in her eyes and held onto every word she said. I was falling in love.

Lisa had recognized me that day in The Trace restaurant because almost a year earlier I had seen her somewhere else.

Greg McDowell and I were on a motorcycle ride one day and while barreling down the highway he yelled over to me, "Wanna go to a party?" I yelled back, "Sure!" He motioned for us to take the next exit ramp at White Bridge Road and led us over to the Rock Harbor Marina on the Cumberland River.

When we arrived, Greg told me he knew a girl that was going to a birthday party on a yacht and had invited him to go. I listened while I followed him down to the docks and we looked for the party. We could see a big yacht pulling out of the cove with a large group of people on it, and we knew that we had missed the party.

We both kicked the gravel in frustration but then saw this guy cleaning the inside of his speed boat. I said, "Hey man, if I give you a little cash would you mind taking us out to that boat?" Without hesitation he said, "Jump in!"

We sped down the river and caught up to the party and waved them down to ask if we could board. They slowed down so we could climb up the side and over the rail to the group. It was quite an entrance if I say so myself. I had no idea at the time that it was Lisa Stewart's birthday party.

I knew who Lisa was since we both were in the music industry but we agreed later that we probably had never met in person until that day, unless it had been at a celebrity function. I was seeing Tiffany at the time and Lisa was on the boat with a boyfriend so we didn't have any connection whatsoever that day. We hung out and chatted a bit but that was about it.

Lisa was a little older than me but not by much, just a year. Her mom and dad were church goers. She told me childhood stories about her family visiting different churches in Mississippi where she would get up and sing. That sounded so familiar, reminding me of when I was a kid. I loved the fact that she knew The Lord and was a believer.

When Lisa moved to Nashville, she secured a record deal at BNA Records and released a couple of singles. Her voice reminded me of a classic 1960s country female singer, like a cross between Tammy Wynette and Patsy Cline. Her voice had a beautiful tone. Lisa put out two singles that charted but didn't get a lot of airplay. She and I both could relate about how our record companies had failed us.

She went on to appear on several television shows in Nashville. She even started hosting shows on The Nashville Network called *Yesteryear* and *This Week In Country Music*. In my opinion, that's where she shone. Lisa had a wonderful speaking voice and she seemed very comfortable in front of a television camera.

I wanted to take her out on our first date to a restaurant called The Blue Moon Waterfront Grill at the Rock Harbor Marina but it was closed that night. Instead, I took her to another romantic restaurant in the Green Hills neighborhood of Nashville. That night was the start of a three-year dating period that eventually led to marriage vows.

Overall Lisa and I were great together. I told her within the first month of dating that I was looking to settle down and have children. She seemed to love that idea as well. I did worry that she was in the entertainment world since the business can be extremely hard on relationships.

Many of my artist friends went through divorces. With so much time spent apart, cheating was the leading cause of marriage breakdowns. Lisa convinced me that she was finished with touring and wanted to stay in Nashville and work as an actress and voiceover artist.

She said her goal was to land a local television hosting job, which I thought was perfect.

I told her I wanted to cut back on touring as well and that it had really taken its toll on me in the past. When I dated Tiffany, it was so hard to really dive into the relationship because I was busy all the time making music and traveling. I knew that it was now time to figure out how to stay at home more.

Mom and Dad really liked Lisa. Mom felt that Lisa was a classy lady and Mom's approval made me happy. Dad told me that he was glad that I found someone that was so compatible with me. However, that didn't mean the first year or so of dating was easy. She and I had our ups and downs. We'd break up for silly little things and then get back together. Both of us were scared, I guess. She had been engaged before and so had I, to Tiffany. We wanted to make sure that everything in our relationship was spot on before moving forward together. But every time we'd break up, I realized more and more that I loved her.

She was spending a lot of time over at my place and we started to discuss her moving in. When we met, I was still renovating my house and finishing up *Thompson Street*. She learned more about me and my history as time went on. I told her about my old relationships and drove her out to Bellevue and to Erin, to show her where I used to live.

I remember one specific moment that never really left me, when visiting my old cabin. When we arrived, I noticed that the new owners weren't at the house so I felt like it'd be okay for us to take a stroll in the woods where the hornet episode took place. While out walking,

I advised Lisa to walk slow and stay behind me because there might be snakes. I had seen a snake in that vicinity before, because it was close to the creek. Donnie Pate had even told me when I moved in that there were a lot of rattlesnakes around there.

Instead of listening to me and walking slowly, I remember Lisa saying something like, "I've been in the country, I know what to look for." She just walked right ahead of me at a fast pace with no regard for my warning. I knew right then that Lisa was an independent woman and she marched to her own drum. All I was trying to do was protect her, but I think she took offense to me advising her.

Over time I discovered that Lisa was her own woman and she did things how she wanted to do them. On one hand, I admired her tenacity and on the other, I was tentative. I loved the fact that she wasn't afraid of stepping out on her own, but I wanted a partner that would trust in me, knowing that I would look out for her and try to protect her.

She was also a chameleon. Lisa had the ability to fit into any crowd. She could walk into a ballroom and socialize with big wig city folk or have a conversation and blend in with the most backwoods country people you can think of. It was hard getting to really know her because she had so many sides.

When I met Lisa's parents, I could tell that they were Godly people and that gave me comfort. We all seemed to have the same religious and political views. I didn't really think they liked me though. Lisa's mother, Earline was a tall, domineering woman and I could tell she could be intimidating to some. She was very stern and not to be messed with. Frank, her dad, was a kind hearted man and just rolled with the punches, I really enjoyed his company. Earline was the pianist in the little Baptist church that they could walk to from their house and Frank was a deacon.

Lisa and I waited for the right love to come along and we would openly talk about the possibility of getting married in front of our families. Everyone seemed to be good with it, even Earline, and that felt good. We both felt like it was time for the next phase of our lives.

I took Lisa out one night and I had planned on taking her to the same little romantic place in Green Hills where we had our first date. We made our way up to the restaurant's door when I realized that it had gone out of business. I was so disappointed. Secretly, I had been planning that day to ask Lisa to marry me that night and now the place was shut down! After pulling on the door handle three or four times to make sure they were closed I turned to Lisa and said, "I'm so sorry!" I dropped to one knee and told her "I can't wait any more, will you marry me?"

She cried and that made me tear up, and then she said yes. We hugged and kissed and I felt like it was almost a good thing that the store had closed. It was like a sign to me. My old life was now behind me. That door had closed and life with Lisa was beginning.

When we got back to the car, she called her parents and told them I asked her to marry me, and that she said yes. They seemed genuinely happy and congratulated us. When she was talking to them, I felt bad that I hadn't called Lisa's father to get his permission. I just assumed he'd be okay with it since we had discussed it many times in front of her parents. Years later I apologized to him for not doing that though. I told him I was just so excited and nervous. It was a spur of the moment thing, and I just had to ask her that night. He was kind and said he completely understood and let me know it was alright with him.

Lisa and I had been looking feverishly to find a new place to live. We finally settled on a place in Cool Springs, close to Franklin, which is about 20 miles south of Nashville. It was a big house in a brand-new subdivision and seemed like a perfect place to start a family.

I never really did much with my real estate license. I did however use it to sell my house on Cedar Lane and buy the new house in Franklin. I made the commission on my fixer upper in Hillsboro Village and also got the commission on the new house. So in the end, I saved about twenty-thousand dollars. That was worth two weeks of sitting in a classroom and paying fifteen hundred dollars for the twenty-thousand-dollar discount.

When planning for the wedding, Lisa and I decided that we'd just invite our friends and family to Franklin and have the ceremony in the living room by the fireplace. We hired a wedding planner and asked our friend Dan Grimes to film it. He set up a monstrous camera jib by the stairs. It looked like a Hollywood film crew was there. My brother Greg was ordained in Ohio as a minister, just so he could marry us in front of approximately fifty loved-ones. It was a wonderful and simple ceremony. Lisa looked beautiful.

A funny thing happened that evening. You see, Lisa's last name is Stewart which means she's of Scottish descent. She thought it would be cool to have a guy playing the bagpipe while she walked down the staircase with Frank. We wanted it to be a surprise for everyone.

It was certainly a surprise to my dad. When that guy blew that first big long note Dad thought the fire alarm went off. There were candles lit all around the house and Dad thought something was on fire. Luckily, he didn't react too abruptly. He realized pretty quickly what was going on and stayed next to me at the front of the room.

We had our reception in a big tent beside our house. We cut the cake and danced. We spent the night at a local hotel and flew out the next morning to spend our honeymoon in Las Vegas at the Bellagio. Lisa and I spent the next several years enjoying spending time with one another and loving married life in our new home.

I had waited for thirty years and I felt like God had filled my heart with love. I took the words "to have and to hold from this day forward; for better, for worse, for richer, for poorer, in sickness and in health, to love and to cherish, till death do us part" very seriously. I felt it was the most important vow that I would make to Lisa and God during my lifetime. I felt completely secure that I could and would abide by those words, and I did.

THE DIVINE MARRIAGE

Marriage is a blessing from God. "*So God created man in his own image, in the image of God created he him; male and female created he them. And God blessed them, and God said unto*

them, Be fruitful, and multiply, and replenish the earth, and subdue it: and have dominion over the fish of the sea, and over the fowl of the air, and over every living thing that moveth upon the earth."
-Genesis 1:27-28 KJV

With great power comes great responsibility. I know, I know...that's a quote from Spiderman, but it's true with God's blessings too. The biblical version is, *"For unto whomsoever much is given, of him shall be much required."*
-Luke 12:48 KJV

We have the responsibility as Christians to do our research about making an oath to God and to our soon to be marriage partner. Too often couples rush into marriage without praying and seeking God's guidance first. If I had to do it all over again, I would've sought out a premarital counselor for Lisa and I to consult with or would've gone to a marriage seminar or retreat.

I would've done everything possible to make sure I was prepared for the complexities and intricacies of wedlock. I can't stress enough how difficult times can be during a marriage. If you think it's bad while you're dating, just wait until you're married! When you say those vows, you and your mate become one. From then on out you can't just go off and do what you want when times get hard. You have to endure it together. Sacrifice from both parties will need to be made each and every day.

If you want a happy and fulfilling marriage, I would encourage you to invite Jesus into your heart and home. Pray for thoughtfulness, kindness, forgiveness, patience and selfishness on a daily basis. Let Him and the Word govern your decisions and conversations. Don't just go on your instincts, they can lead you down a road that could be a dead end. We as humans are not capable of seeing our relationships from a birds-eye view like God can. He can keep us from perilous situations.

Loyalty has also got to be at the forefront of your union. Do not let Satan step into your inner circle. Temptation is around every corner, especially when the newness of your love wears off. The devil will do everything he can do to undo what God brought together. Know he is at work and don't fall for his lies. Remember that love is not just a word, it's an action and choice.

My advice would be, both you and your partner study the Word to see what God's marriage rules and recommendations are. Don't say those vows until both of you are in complete agreement. There is no turning back once they're said. Once you do, follow those rules. Stay vigilant and work on your marriage as though you would a job. Make it successful!

And lastly...happiness will come and go. Don't base your relationship on it. There will be days when it's pure bliss and then they'll be days so bad you'll wanna pull your hair out. Sometimes months or even years of bad times! But guess what, that's what you signed up for. Unhappiness doesn't get you a free card to get divorced. It's your job to fix the issue or endure the darkness until the sun comes out.

Don't be embarrassed to get help if things get really bad. Seek out Christian counseling. Ask your Christian friends or church members to give you advice on who to speak with. There are many resources out there to assist you.

I speak from experience here; expectations can be devastating to your marriage. Happiness should come from God first. Too many times we expect our partner to give it to us. We're humans, He's God! He can give it to us. He can calm the storms, we can't. When we have a strong relationship with God, then there's nothing we can't accomplish in our relationships. Let Him fix the issues you have. Learn from His sacrifice on the cross and His never-ending forgiveness of us and apply it to your marriage.

"Wives, submit yourselves to your own husbands as you do to the Lord. For the husband is the head of the wife as Christ is the head of the church, his body, of which he is the Savior. Now as the church submits to Christ, so also wives should submit to their husbands in everything. Husbands, love your wives, just as Christ loved the church and gave himself up for her to make her holy, cleansing her by the washing with water through the word, and to present her to himself as a radiant church, without stain or wrinkle or any other blemish, but holy and blameless. In this same way, husbands ought to love their wives as their own bodies. He who loves his wife loves himself. After all, no one ever hated their own body, but they feed and care for their body, just as Christ does the church—for we are members of his body. For this reason a man will leave his father and mother and be united to his wife, and the two will become one flesh. This is a profound mystery—but I am talking about Christ and the church. However, each one of you also must love his wife as he loves himself, and the wife must respect her husband." -Ephesians 5:22-33 NIV

Chapter Ten:
Big White Horse

"To everything there is a season, and a time for every purpose under the heaven: A time to be born, and a time to die; a time to plant and a time to pluck up that which is planted."
-Ecclesiastes 3:1-2 KJV

The year was 2004. Mark Zuckerberg launched a social media site called thefacebook.com. Everyone was still using their cell *phones* for just that...calling people. No one was texting. When people socialized, they actually went outside to do it.

I forget exactly how I ran into Del Gray that year but I know that he had a publishing deal with Charlie Daniels' company. While I was out socializing, somehow or the other Del and I met up through an acquaintance that worked there. I think I may have been making rounds around town to see if I could get a publishing deal as a songwriter.

We hadn't talked in years, but we seemed to pick up right where we left off. We didn't talk much about me leaving the band or why I left. It was just good to see him again. I felt like enough time had gone by to just let it go.

The two of us, along with O'Brien and Propes met up at Del's publishing company and talked for about an hour or so to see if we could all get on the same page with one another. The meeting went well and everyone was cordial and kind.

They were wondering if Porter would be interested at all in the possibility of a reunion and I told them I sincerely thought he'd want to. Not long after that I called Porter and sure enough, he was open to discussing it. The only missing factor now was Tim.

I think Propes called him first asking what he thought and Tim wasn't interested. There had been too much water under the bridge, I guess. I wasn't privy to what happened between him and the guys after I left. All I knew was that there had been some heated discussions and even physical altercations on the bus.

When the band split up in 1997, Tim was signed as a solo artist at Atlantic Records. He released a couple of singles that did pretty well, and had the same kind of success as my solo projects. In 2003 he formed a group called Rushlow, which was Tim and five other musicians, including his cousin Doni Harris. They were signed to Lyric Street Records and put out a top twenty single called "I Can't Be Your Friend." The label folded soon after, and Tim was available to pursue another musical project, if he wanted to.

So we were all disappointed that he wasn't into the idea of us getting back together. I remember calling Tim trying to convince him that the reunion would be incredible for us to do. But no matter what I said he wasn't budging from his position.

He did tell me some of the things that were said to him. Some of the allegations made against him were pretty shocking. I've decided not to share those things in the book because that's his business, not mine. But after he told me his side of the story, I completely understood his reasoning.

After speaking with Tim, I was hesitant about moving forward with the band. But I reasoned that the negative stuff was behind us now, and everyone deserves a second chance. I was also excited to see what we'd sound like again. We had arranged a time to rehearse at Del's house, up in his bonus room. The idea was for me to front the band, but have Porter and O'Brien step up and sing lead every now and then.

Porter and I started writing to see if we could come up with some new tunes to record and came up with one in particular called, "Hello Again." It was a rocker. The lyrics told the story of our band and how we were happy to be back at it.

Six or seven months before the guys and I started talking, I had struck up a friendship with Heartbreaker, Stan Lynch. As in, Tom Petty and The Heartbreakers. We connected through Rod Parkin, a song plugger that worked for a publishing company called Peermusic. I met him while searching for a publishing deal one day, and he was adamant about Stan and I meeting. He felt we'd get along great. Well of course I was flattered and told him I'd be honored to speak with him.

When Stan and I talked it was as if we were family. We had the same mannerisms, the same way of describing things, and more importantly, the same musical tastes. Stan was a Buckeye, just like me. We both were from Ohio.

I knew Stan was not only an incredible drummer and singer but he was a stellar songwriter and producer. He had produced acts like the Eagles, Don Henley and The Band. He had recently been inducted into The Rock & Roll Hall of Fame, in 2002.

I thought he'd be the perfect producer for the new sound of Little Texas. I asked the guys, and they were up for me calling him to see if he'd be interested. I made the call and Stan was extremely cool with it. He said, "Dude, I'd love to give it a try. Just buy me a plane ticket and a cheap hotel room and I'll be there."

And that's exactly what we did. We flew him in several weeks later and booked the big room at OmniSound Studios. Stan and I both had recorded there before and we loved how rock and roll it sounded. They had a killer API recording console in there that sounded amazing.

The tracking of the song went perfectly but when it came time to overdub, it quickly went awry. Porter brought his guitar into the control room with Stan and the engineer to really dive into the parts he wanted on the final track. For some reason Porter and Stan didn't get along. Maybe it was Stan's forwardness and honesty or maybe Porter just didn't like his ideas. In the end, Porter wasn't happy with how things turned out.

When it came time for me to sing lead, I took a computer monitor in the vocal booth and recorded myself on Pro Tools. I told everyone that I'd try to get a really good track first, and then I'd see what everyone thought. Well once I was done, I brought Porter in first, just because he was the closest one to the booth, to have him listen. After he listened all he could say was, "That didn't register on my cool meter."

I didn't say anything, even though I was offended. Maybe Porter was still reeling and perturbed about the run-in with Stan, so I just let it be. When I brought Stan in to listen, he loved it. I was confused as to why there were two very different opinions about my vocal track. I told Stan I'd change a few things I felt like Porter wanted me to work on, and left it at that. The other guys didn't say much when they heard it. I didn't feel the love, for sure. O'Brien and Propes sang their parts and we finished up the session.

After being in the studio, I was feeling very doubtful about my role as the new lead singer. I didn't feel that Porter and the guys had a lot of confidence in me. None of them really seemed to care for the track or working with a Rock and Roll Hall of Famer such as Stan. I started to second guess whether or not to move forward with the reunion.

Right around that same time the band got a letter from Tim and Jeff Huskins' attorney wanting us to stop the progression of the band. They felt like they were owed something for being members of the band. This didn't sit well with me at all. I called Tim to hear his side of the story and he said he felt like he helped build the trademark and Jeff had too. He said that he and Jeff wanted a percentage of everything we did as a band, for a period of time.

I told him, "Tim I never took a dime when I left Little Texas, I walked away on my own accord because it was my decision." I told him that I didn't think it was fair to pay him and Jeff something when they were deciding not to be in the new formation of the band. In my own mind I didn't think it was right that I'd personally have to pay him and Jeff money when I wasn't paid one dime when I left.

Not only did I not ask for any future royalties, I signed over my rights to the name Little Texas. I was the one leaving, it was my decision! Why would I make them pay me money? I didn't see the logic. Yes, I helped build the name and yes, my face was on the covers of the records and CDs, but I was the one leaving. Me!

The guys were very upset that Jeff and Tim would ask that of us but somehow or the other reasoned that it'd be worth it to pay them just so we could go and work. I disagreed completely. I put my foot down and said no. I was not willing to do that. I told them that the only way I'd agree to this lunacy was for all of them to pay me a percentage for their past performance and concession profits.

They turned on me and became angry. I didn't really expect them to pay me, I just wanted them to realize how unfair this was to me. We got into a big heated argument at Del's house and at some point, I stormed out, never to return again. They didn't see my side at all. They couldn't see how I'd feel the way I did and it hurt...again!

Luckily, I had another plan in action. I had been contemplating putting another band together after the incident with Stan at Omni. A band that would appreciate what I brought to the table. One where the members got along and there was no jealousy or animosity.

I never hid it from the Little Texas guys either. I was completely up front with the guys about the possibility of my other musical projects. They were totally fine with it. Porter was also in another band called Hilljack at the time and Del had a side band that he was in as well. O'Brien and Propes also had other ventures in the works.

I had been thinking about a four-piece country band made up of veteran players. I knew I wanted Trey Landry in the band. Trey had been playing drums for me for a couple of solo shows and he was a groove machine. He was from Louisiana and knew how to lay back on the beat. He always played what was right for the song, not just to show off.

The other guy I knew I wanted to be in the band was Mark "Sparky" Matejka. He had also played with me as a solo artist and I was extremely impressed by him. He had played with the band Sons of The Desert and with Charlie Daniels. Not only could Sparky play superbly, but he could also sing.

The only thing that was missing was a great bass player. The three of us started putting out the word on the street to see if we could find someone to fill the last remaining position in the band. After several months of looking, we were all getting nervous that we may not find the right guy.

Right around that same time Lisa ran into an old record producer she knew named Richard Landis. Recently, I reached out to him to see what he remembered about how we all hooked up. Here's what he had to say...

Some time ago (I cannot remember the time frame), I was sitting in a jeep, waiting to cross Cool Springs Blvd, in the Franklin area of TN...the sky had opened up, and it was like a monsoon. I looked to my left, and saw 2 women walking down the blvd, huddled under a single raincoat that was over their heads, and getting drenched. As they got closer, I recognized Lisa Stewart and her Mom. Lisa had been a recording artist on BNA when I was the head of A&R there. I signed her, and produced an album on her and got to know her Mom as well. As they approached, I honked the horn, and waved. They ran to my car and got in. After all the greetings, we drove across to PF Chang's for a bite, and caught up. Lisa told me that she was engaged, and before she could tell me anything more about it, I told her to book a dinner, and introduce me to her fiancé.

A couple of weeks later, she called, and suggested Margot's, *in East Nashville. My ex and I got there early, and then I saw Lisa enter with Brady Seals, whom I recognized from Little Texas. We didn't know each other, but I'd seen him at some industry functions. We dined, and he asked me what I was up to. I'd just moved back from FL, and as a favor to Lorrie Morgan, a regular production client of mine, I did a spec project on her new husband, Sammy Kershaw. Brady told me he'd been writing with Rodney Crowell. So, we all decided that after dinner, we'd go to the studio I was renting in Berry Hill, called Blueberry Hill. The four of us went, and I played Brady an odd, quite modern (for Country) track I'd done on Sammy. He was impressed. He then played me a song or two he'd just written, and I was impressed…so, we discussed working together. He told me he wanted to be in a band, and not a solo act. But he didn't have a band so he was going to audition players, and try to put one together.*

I figured I'd never hear from him again.

Several weeks later, Brady called and told me he had everything in place, except a bass player, and that he was auditioning at his house and invited me over. The first, and only bass player I heard, was the remarkable Keith Horne, who also sang high parts, and played breakneck speed acoustic guitar as well…so, we now had a band.

I had 1 song in my pocket, and Brady had 2 …so, I took them into Blueberry Hill, and cut 3 songs. They came out fantastic. At the time, I was partners with James Stroud on a studio called Loud Recording. James had produced Little Texas in the past, and was the head of the DreamWorks label in Nashville. I told him I had something he had to hear. When he heard it was a band, he said "forget it. I don't need another band." I persisted. I took Brady over to Loud, played James one song. He lit up, and told us we had a deal.

That was the birth of Hot Apple Pie.

I feel I need to expand on the last remaining member of the band…I got a call on the phone one day just out of the blue and it was Keith Horne. I said, "Is this THE Keith Horne?" He laughed and so did I. I couldn't believe he had called me. I thought for sure he'd have a road gig with a major recording artist. Everyone in town knew how incredible Keith was. He had played with all kinds of predominant artists. Artists like Peter Frampton, Trisha Yearwood, Tanya Tucker, Chaka Khan and many others. He said that he had heard through the grapevine that we were looking for a bass player, that could sing and he'd like to throw his name in that hat.

I invited him over to jam with me and the boys. We knew after the first verse that he was our guy. I knew in my heart and soul that we were going to do something great with this lineup. Now that we had a producer, and a place to record, all we needed was a killer name. We needed to take some cool pictures and record some truly memorable songs and we'd be ready for the big leagues.

Hot Apple Pie in Nashville, TN (First Photo Shoot)
From left to right: Mark "Sparky" Matejka, Brady Seals, Trey Landry and Keith Horne
Photo Credit: Lisa Stewart

Hot Apple Pie in Nashville, TN (First Photo Shoot)
From left to right: Keith Horne, Mark "Sparky" Matejka, Trey
Landry and Brady Seals

I started with the name. I had been listening to nothing but The Band and The Beatles around that time and every time I would think about a name, I would think of Apple Records, the recording company that The Beatles started. Even though it was an English company, I loved how country their little green apple icon was.

One night in the bathtub, brainstorming with Lisa, I was considering the names The Apples, The Little Green Apples, The Juicy Apples, The Baked Apples...when Lisa said The Hot Apples. I immediately thought...Hot Apple Pie! It seemed perfect. I thought it was a perfect name for a country band. It reminded me of home. I loved that it evoked a sense of taste and smell. I also loved the subtle relation to the old rock band, Humble Pie.

The guys loved it too. We all knew that we weren't going to beat that name. Once we knew our name, the direction of the band started to become clearer. We all loved The Band, The Eagles, Jackson Brown and anything that was authentic and earthy. We started rehearsing songs by The Band like "The Weight" and "Shape I'm In." It felt incredible.

I was writing non-stop; Rodney Crowell and I had finished a song called "Annabelle (Arkansas Is Calling You)" that was a staple for the sound of the project. Some other writers that helped make the project special were Mike Reid, Jeffery Steele, Al Anderson, Gordon Bradberry, Dennis Robbins and Andrew Dorff, Michel Dulaney, Steven Dale Jones, Jason Sellers, Greg McDowell, my uncle Troy and my cousin TJ.

I have vivid memories of the day Troy, Gordon and I wrote the song, "Slowin' Down The Fall." After we finished it, I remember saying, "Dang, we need to pitch this to Willie Nelson, it sounds just like something he'd do." It was a slow country classic.

When I played it to the guys, they loved it too. Richard agreed that it sounded like a Willie song. I suggested to him how I'd love to get Willie to come in and make a guest appearance on the record. We loved the idea and got to work trying to make it happen.

I had an old friend named Steven "Herky" Williams that worked at ASCAP. He and I had been playing a little golf together every now and then. The dude was a killer golfer, but what was more impressive about him was the people he knew. One day I called Herky to see if he might be able to pull some strings and ask Willie if he'd want to sing on our record.

Several weeks later he called and said that Willie was going to be recording in Nashville and he'd be hanging out with him all day. I asked Herky to find out what studio Willie was going to be in so we could rent a studio that was close by. That way it'd be easy for him to come over and overdub his vocal.

We devised a plan where Richard and I rented the studio right behind where Herky and Willie were going to be. It was Loud Recording. All Willie would have to do is walk across the alleyway, right into where we were. It was a long shot but if it worked, it would pay off big time.

I talked to Herky several times that day and he'd give me updates about Willie's whereabouts. He told me it'd be around 6:00 pm, if it was going to happen at all. So we waited...and waited...and then finally Herky called me and said, "Willie's on his way". I panicked! I couldn't believe this was actually going to happen.

About fifteen minutes later he walked through the door. Him and Herky. I probably looked like a cat that just ate a bird. I didn't know what to do. I was starstruck. Somehow though, I kept my composure. I put out my hand to Willie and he shook it. I told him who I was and why we had asked him to come there.

I informed him that I was related to Troy Seals and he immediately let down his guard. He and Troy had been friends for a very long time. In fact, I discovered later that Troy had flown to Vegas back in the '90s to write with Willie and Waylon. They all stayed in a hotel and wrote several songs together that appeared on a duet record that Willie and Waylon put out called, *Clean Shirt*.

I told Willie that Troy and I along with Gordon Bradberry wrote a song called "Slowin' Down The Fall." I told him that Troy and I both thought it sounded like a song he'd sing. Willie said something like, "Well let's go hear it then."

We made our way into the control room to listen. I remember Willie sitting down in the producer's chair, right in front of the console, and I was right behind him. The engineer, Rick Cobble pushed play. I had already sung Willie's parts on the recording so he could hear what it should sound like.

Then, one of the greatest musical moments in my life happened. When the song was done, Willie turned to me and said, "Now that's a great song," I could've died and gone to honky-tonk heaven right there. I thanked him and we started on the track.

We all discussed which verses he'd sing and what he should do on the chorus. When he made his way into the vocal booth to sing, I was just ecstatic. I was sitting there listening to Willie sing one of my songs! God is good.

I remember one incident at the end of the session that was extremely embarrassing though. I had gotten a little carried away with the producer role when I asked Willie, "Do you think maybe you could sing that last line like this?"...and then I proceeded to sing the line as we had written it. Willie said in a calm but matter of fact way, "I like it just the way it is." I fumbled around and pushed the talk button and said with an uncomfortable laugh, "Me too, never mind what I said." I thought to myself, "What the heck are you thinking Seals! That's Willie Nelson!"

When we finished his overdub, he came in and listened. It sounded perfect. He was as kind as a man could be. I think he really liked it too. We shook hands and made our way to the door. I told him that it was so good to meet him and then jokingly said, "The only thing that would make this meeting a little better would be a big joint." He said without a pause, "I have one right here." Then he reached into his coat pocket and pulled out a tightly rolled Bob Marley cigarette. We all stood there at the door and passed it around. I hadn't smoked in years but I figured I would one last time, with Willie.

Willie Nelson and Brady Seals
Photo Credit: Lisa Stewart

When searching for songs for the HAP (Hot Apple Pie) record I stumbled on one that caught everyone's ears. TJ, Greg and I had written it years prior when I lived in Bellevue...way before Hot Apple Pie was even a thought. It was called "Hillbillies Love It In The Hay". It had a bouncy little Bo Diddley groove and was just crazy enough to be a contender.

I remember going in for the first time to meet everyone at DreamWorks Records to play some of the songs we had recorded. It all felt so familiar. I met with Scott Borchetta who I had known for years. He was Head of Promotion. We rode Harleys together down in Daytona, back when I was with Little Texas. Christy DiNapoli and Scott had been good friends for years. George Briner was there too. He was a radio promoter. I'd known George from the Warner Bros. days. Bruce Shindler was there as well. He used to be one of the biggest independent radio promoters in town. I had worked with him for years.

And of course, there was James Stroud. James was Little Texas' producer. He and I always got along and he was fun to be around. I was so excited to meet everyone else that worked for the company too. I really felt like this ride was going to send the band to the top. It was a strong team and everyone seemed to genuinely love our music.

Another memorable musical moment happened around about that time that didn't have anything to do with Hot Apple Pie. It was when Dobie Gray sang a song, I co-wrote with TJ called, "Say It." I grew up listening to Dobie's records and I wore out his album, *Drift Away* when I was a kid. I remember my dad telling me that

Troy was really good friends with him, and so in a way he felt like family.

I'd later find out that he and Troy often frequented the same recording studio in Nashville that was owned by David Briggs and Norbert Putnam called Quadraphonic Sound Studio. That place was bangin' out the hits in the '70s. Neil Young's *Harvest Moon* was recorded there for God's sake.

I can't remember exactly how it all happened but TJ or Troy had played our song to Dobie and he loved it. TJ called me one day and told me that Dobie was looking for songs for his new record and I was ecstatic at the possibility that Dobie would cut our song.

The song was reminiscent of something dramatic singers like Roy Orbison or K.D. Lang would sing. The track we recorded was very sparse and featured just a guitar, accordion and mandolin. The lyrics of the song gave the listener advice about how it's important not to wait to say how you feel about someone you love. "Before it's too late…say it".

I got the call one day and it was Dobie on the other end. We scheduled a time for him to come over to my home studio and record his vocal on the tracks we already had. Several weeks later he rang my doorbell.

He was such a sweet soul and so incredibly kind. He was very complimentary of the song and decided it'd be a perfect fit for his new project. I sat there with headphones on and engineered him overdubbing his vocal. I couldn't believe what I was hearing. Dobie Gray…in my house…singing a song I co-wrote. It was surreal.

Dobie never got around to making another record. He was featured on Uncle Kracker's version of "Drift Away," but that was the last time he was heard on radio. Dobie died from cancer on December 6th, 2011.

I had so many wonderful things that were happening to me during those years it was hard to keep up with the blessings. Being able to meet some of my musical heroes and have them sing on my songs was sublime. Plus to have another record deal, wow!...I was so grateful. God had sat me back in the saddle once again on a big white horse to take another ride. And to top it all off, I was happily married. It was all God. I was as thankful as a man could be.

GOD'S PERFECT WILL

Pray for God's Will to be done every time you pray. I've done it all of my life. He knows which path is best for all of us. There may be times when one door closes and another one opens. Sometimes that's good in the moment, and sometimes it seems bad. It seemed bad for me that God closed the door to re-forming Little Texas, but it turned out to be good. He blessed me by giving me a record deal with Hot Apple Pie.

The scriptures speak of doors being closed through God, but opened another way for things to work, by His Perfect Will. Remember them and know that your path is laid by the Almighty God.

"And to the angel of the church in Philadelphia write; These things saith he that is holy, he that is true, he that hath the key of

David, he that openeth, and no man shutteth; and shutteth, and no man openeth; I know thy works: behold, I have set before thee an open door, and no man can shut it: for thou hast a little strength, and hast kept my word, and hast not denied my name." -Revelation 3:7-8 KJV

With the help of the Holy Spirits' whispers and nudges, God is causing all things to work together for our ultimate good. Not everything turns out like we envision though. Hard lessons may have to be learned. Maybe God's intent is for us to get closer to Him. Or maybe God wants our story to encourage someone else in their crisis that's more dire than ours. Adversity is a tried and true method of building character. Ask any United States Marine and they'll agree. In the end, we become resilient soldiers for His mission.

"Put on the whole armour of God, that ye may be able to stand against the wiles of the devil.

For we wrestle not against flesh and blood, but against principalities, against powers, against the rulers of the darkness of this world, against spiritual wickedness in high places.

Wherefore take unto you the whole armour of God, that ye may be able to withstand in the evil day, and having done all, to stand.

Stand therefore, having your loins girt about with truth, and having on the breastplate of righteousness;

And your feet shod with the preparation of the gospel of peace;

Above all, taking the shield of faith, wherewith ye shall be able to quench all the fiery darts of the wicked.

And take the helmet of salvation, and the sword of the Spirit, which is the word of God:" -Ephesians 6:11-17 KJV

Chapter Eleven:
Sugar Momma

"If ye abide in me, and my words abide in you, ye shall ask what ye will, and it shall be done unto you." -John 15:7 KJV

The label picked "Hillbillies" (Love It In The Hay) to be our first single. It was a crazy little song, but it was memorable. The bass line along with the guitar licks and beat made you want to dance. It wasn't the direction I really wanted to go in, but I trusted those around me and threw caution to the wind.

The label chose a director to film the video and the next thing we knew we were flying to L.A. to shoot it. After we landed, we drove to the canyon. It was beautiful out there. We pulled up to an old barn. Everyone was a delight and the director really seemed like he knew what he was doing.

All was great until we saw the final edit weeks later. I remember all of us sitting around at the label and there was an uncomfortable silence. No one liked it. It was as generic as it could be. There was nothing about it that was special at all. I started to worry. I thought, "Please God, don't let this be our debut video."

He answered my prayer. None of the executives wanted to release it either. The problem was simply that the label just spent a ton of money on nothing. Thank God, Richard and I convinced them of the importance of the band's debut video and the label agreed to finance another one.

It just so happened that one day I was watching music videos at home and saw a Lenny Kravitz video called "Lady" and loved how it was shot. I called Richard and asked if he'd mind if I could call Retta, the production manager at the label and suggest a director. Richard didn't mind at all.

I suggested Philip Andelman. He was mostly a pop director but I thought that was a good thing for that particular song. I wanted to really make the video memorable and edgy. Retta seemed to love the idea and told me to go ahead and reach out to him and see if he'd be interested.

Not only was Philip interested but he was excited. He really liked the fact that he was going to shoot a video for a country band. Once he heard the song, he called the label and they started to work out a time to make it happen.

We shot it in L.A. again. This time it was indoors. Philip had the idea to do a spoof on Snoop Dogg's video "Drop It Like It's Hot". Instead of showing Bentley cars and high dollar yachts, we'd show jacked up trucks and bass boats. It worked like a charm. The simple white background really made the band stand out and the video turned out to be exactly what the band wanted. The label loved it!

We wrapped up the video and set our sights on touring. We needed a manager. Richard Landis and I met with Scott Siman. I had worked with Scott before when he was a music industry attorney. Now he was managing and had his own company called RPM Entertainment. Scott was a major player and everyone knew who he was. He was managing Tim McGraw at the time and I felt like he'd be a great asset to the band.

He seemed to really love the music and our musical direction. I guess it didn't hurt for us to already have a deal, thanks to Richard. Scott along with CAA would later pull some strings and send Hot Apple Pie out on the road with Tim McGraw and Keith Urban.

From left to right: Trey Landry, Brady Seals, Tim McGraw, Mark "Sparky" Matejka and Keith Horne
Photo Credit: Lisa Stewart

The single came out of the box screamin'. At the time we broke a record as being the highest debuting country band. The video also went on to become "VH1's Sexiest Video." We were all ridin' high. We were out doing a bunch of shows across the country. The band on stage was a powerhouse.

I would switch up and play keyboards, harmonica, guitar and bass. Sparky would play guitar and banjo, Trey would play drums and accordion and Keith would play bass, acoustic guitar and pedal steel. All of us sang.

I think the coolest part of being in HAP was that our peers valued what we were doing. I remember when we opened for Keith Urban, he stood on the side of the stage along with his whole band and watched our show. It was an incredible feeling knowing that other artists appreciated the band.

Hot Apple Pie
From left to right: Keith Horne, Brady Seals, Trey Landry and
Mark "Sparky" Matejka

Hot Apple Pie
Brady Seals and Mark "Sparky" Matejka

In fact, every time we'd play a show with Keith Urban, he and I would hang out a little. I had known Keith since the days when he was in the band The Ranch. I called him once after leaving Little Texas to see if he'd come play guitar for me. He kindly turned me down because he said he was working on a new solo project. I think he made the right choice!

He and I were also writing with some of the same people around that time, My uncle Troy and my producer Rodney Crowell. One fond memory I have is when he and I were asked to film some short segments at the Harley Davidson factory in Milwaukee for a television show. Harley lent us a couple of bikes to ride and Keith and I spent the day in the wind and shooting pool at a little bar along the way.

149

Several new groups come to mind that were being introduced to the public around the same time as HAP. Sugarland, Keith Anderson, Little Big Town and Jason Aldean. All of the new artists would find ourselves playing New Artist events together a lot. The one that stood out the most was Taylor Swift. I was very impressed that she was writing her own material. She was young and pretty and she made a big splash early on.

Every day was filled with adventure when on the road with HAP. I was able to perform in all of the same kind of venues I did with Little Texas. Getting to shake hands and meet up with old fans and friends again was really cool.

A couple of old friends came to see the band when we played a little honky-tonk in Virginia. I had just walked off the stage from doing a soundcheck when in walked my old bus driver, Coma. He looked good and had not changed much. He was still a big ole boy and he still had his red beard.

He really embraced his infamous nickname "Coma" because he had it written in white on his black trucker hat. He had his son Buck with him and a girl friend of theirs named Andrea. We hugged and laughed and exchanged a few inside jokes from the past.

Coma asked, "Where ya stayin'?" I said, "The Red Roof Inn just down the road." He shook his head and said, "That's where we're stayin', you wanna ride with us back to the hotel?" I said, "Sure man, you got room?" He said, "We'll make room."

I headed out the side door with them and hopped in the front seat of their truck. I didn't realize until then that

Buck was going to drive. You see, Buck is a little person and wasn't able to reach the pedals on the floorboard. I looked down and saw three homemade contraptions for his feet. They were made of metal and looked sturdy enough.

Coma and Andrea squeezed into the tiny backseat of the extended cab of the truck. The gadgets that Buck used to operate the vehicle were basically poles that were attached to the gas pedal, brake and clutch. At the top were flat surfaces he could push with his feet and made it to where he could drive the pickup just like a six-foot man, even though he was four feet tall.

I was a little nervous at first, but Buck started it up, pushed the clutch, rammed into reverse, pushed the gas and off we went. He drove that thing just like Coma used to drive our old bus back in the day.

We weren't five miles down the highway when Buck's cell phone rang. He answered and the conversation started, "Hello?" Now the rest of us couldn't hear the other person on the line so we all just sat there and listened to Buck. His voice sounded just like Coma's voice but just a little higher in pitch. He had a thick southern drawl that was nasally and stern sounding. He said, "Hold on, hold on, what do you mean?"

He went on, "You talkin' 'bout that girl that works at Wal-Mart?" I could tell by his tone that he was truly concerned and sincere. "No!, I can't believe it...Oh my God." At this point we knew something was wrong. We all waited in silence to hear what was happening. Buck said, "I'm in the truck with Brady right now, we're drivin' back to the hotel. I'll call you in a minute." And just like that he hung up.

I just sat there not knowing what to say. Buck looked into the rear view mirror and said to Coma, "Daddy, you know that girl at Wal-Mart...she just got shot." Coma said in a mournful way, "Oh no." I had no idea what was happening but I knew something bad just happened.

We all got out and started walkin' towards the hotel. Buck stopped and said, "Go on without me, I'm going to make a phone call." Coma had always had a problem of getting too close to ya when he talked, but this time he was even closer. While we walked Coma whispered... "You know that girl that Buck was talkin' about?" I said, "Yeah man, is everything okay?" He said, "That's his sugar momma."

I said, "What?...what do you mean?" I was confused. I didn't put two and two together. I had no idea what he was talking about. He said it again just a little louder... "That's his sugar momma." I still was in the dark. He could tell I hadn't a clue what he was saying. He went on to say, "She likes little people."

"Her husband probably found out that she's been hanging out with Buck. He's probably the one that shot her." I'm thinking right about then that this is way too crazy for me to be involved with. I'm now wondering if the boyfriend is going to try and come for Buck. Should I be fearing for my life right about now?

Within minutes we made our way into the hotel and Coma lead me to their room. I sat on one bed, he sat at the little table by the AC unit and Andrea lays down on the other bed. Coma was goin' on and on with some other story and I was still in a daze, thinking about an exit strategy.

Then in walks Buck. He says, "Daddy, it was her." Now I knew the backstory and this was not good news. There was this long silent pause and I was thinking that Buck was going to be remorseful or saddened by the tragic event. Instead he said to me, "Brady...I think I want to start a midget band!"

I just sat there in shock for a moment. I didn't know what to say. I was expecting a totally different conversation. I tried to shake it off and go with the flow and I said, "Wow man...really...that's cool." I stuttered and said, "Are you going to be the singer?"

Without missing a beat, he said, "Yeah, I used to sing in high school in Choir class." I shook my head and said, "Alright then...do you have some other little guys you know that can be in your band?" He said he knew a pedal steel player that would probably want to do it.

I tried to envision what that might look like. Since the guy was a little person, I didn't know whether he would cut off the ends of the legs of the steel to play it or whether he'd add extensions to the knee levers and pedals like Buck did to his truck's floor mounts.

I had a light bulb idea, "I got it", I said. You ought to debut it on the Jerry Springer Show. The nationally syndicated show was known to bring on some bizarre guests. It was nothing to see brawls break out on the stage or for there to be situations that would include some kind of physical stunt, such as wrestling in food or contests involving strippers.

I had the idea because Buck had been on there before. Buck was invited to be on the show and pretend he had a fetish for wearing diapers under his pants. It was all made up just for the show, but he had been there and done that.

As soon as I told him my idea Buck shot back, "No man, this is serious." That stopped me in my tracks. I didn't know what to say, I just went with it and said, "Oh okay, I get it." I just let him continue on and told him to call me if something ever happened with it and I would help if I could.

On the other bed, Andrea chimed in and said, "Being on Jerry Springer ain't no big deal." I looked over and said, "Have you been on The Jerry Springer Show before?" She said, "Yeah...they air-brushed my body to make me look like a leopard and I had to waller around in a baby pool full of milk."

My mind was blown. I thought, "What kind of craziness have I gotten myself into!" I can't remember what happened after that, it's all a blur. Every time I ever hung out with Coma and Buck it was pure madness. I could write a book solely on Coma stories.

Dear Heavenly Father

Prayer works! I didn't want that video of "Hillbillies" to be released and neither did God. Whether you're a seasoned Christian or a newcomer to the faith, praying is one of the most important things we need to do. Praying is simply talking to God. Either audibly or just in our minds. He just wants to have a relationship with us.

It's my opinion that prayers can be as simple as just saying one unembellished phrase like "Thank You

Jesus", or "Be with me God". However, when I pray at night or for something special, I always address him first by saying, "Dear Heavenly Father". Next I praise Him and thank Him for all of His blessings and I ask for His Will to be done in my life. After that, I ask for forgiveness for my sins. My personal touch is to end my prayers with saying, "In Jesus' name". I try my best (even though I'm not always successful) to use the prayer template Jesus gave us in the Bible. Otherwise known as The Lord's Prayer.

"After this manner therefore pray ye: Our Father which art in heaven, Hallowed be thy name.

Thy kingdom come, Thy will be done in earth, as it is in heaven.

Give us this day our daily bread.

And forgive us our debts, as we forgive our debtors.

And lead us not into temptation, but deliver us from evil: For thine is the kingdom, and the power, and the glory, for ever. Amen."
-Matthew 6:9-13 KJV

You might ask, "Does He even hear my prayers?" The answer is "Yes!". He's promised in His Word that He hears our prayers. The Psalmist declared, *"As for me, I will call upon God; and the Lord shall save me. Evening, and morning, and at noon, will I pray, and cry aloud: and he shall hear my voice." -Psalm 55:16-17 KJV*

He hears us because Jesus Christ removed the barrier between us and God, a barrier caused by our sins. In the Old Testament of The Bible we didn't have the ability to come before God because of our iniquities. By His death, Jesus died for our sins and removed the barrier to communicate with God. All we have to do is ask to be saved.

No prayer goes unheard when you're a Christian. You just have to ask with the right motives. *"Ye ask, and receive not, because ye ask amiss, that ye may consume it upon your lusts."* *-James 4:3 KJV.* I always ask the Lord to forgive me for my sins when I pray, just to make sure my transgressions don't come between He and I. I also want Him to know I'm sincere and reverent. *"But your iniquities have separated between you and your God, and your sins have hid his face from you, that he will not hear."* *-Isaiah 59:2 KJV.*

The answer to your prayer may be instantaneous or it may take years. And remember, when you say, "Thy Will be done" you're putting it in His hands at that point. His understanding is higher than ours. Your request may not be the best thing for you even though you think it is. Trust in Him.

There are so many ways to approach praying and I urge whomever is reading this right now to dive deep into the scriptures and learn about how to communicate with our Heavenly Father. Get into a good church and ask questions.

The Bible says, *"Let us therefore come boldly unto the throne of grace, that we may obtain mercy, and find grace to help in time of need."* *-Hebrews 4:16 KJV.* If you've never done so, ask Christ to come into your life today. It'll be the most important and rewarding thing you'll ever do.

I believe the late great evangelist, Billy Graham left us a perfect prayer for all sinners. All you have to do is believe it with all your heart and say these simple but powerful words and you will be saved.

"Dear Lord Jesus, I know that I am a sinner, and I ask for Your forgiveness. I believe You died for my sins and rose from the dead. I turn from my sins and invite You to come into my heart and life. I want to trust and follow You as my Lord and Savior. In Your Name."
-Amen

CHAPTER TWELVE:
ONE MORE DAY IN HEAVEN

*"I call heaven and earth to record this day against you, that I have
set before you life and death, blessing and cursing: therefore choose
life, that both thou and thy seed may live:"*
-Deuteronomy 30:19 KJV

Hot Apple Pie was shooting up the charts when
we got the news that Scott Borchetta was
leaving the label. I was devastated. Deep down
I knew that it was the beginning of the end for the label
and the band. Scott was the best of the best. He was
the big reason that DreamWorks was having the success
they were having at country radio. There was no one
that could replace him. He left and took Toby Keith with
him, DreamWorks' top-selling artist.

Hot Apple Pie had barely built up steam when the
bottom fell out. I couldn't believe what I was hearing.
Richard, along with James Stroud, tried to reassure me
that everything would be alright. But I knew it wouldn't
be. The talk in Nashville was not Hot Apple Pie, it was
Scott Borchetta leaving to start up a company called Big
Machine Records. Their first artist to be signed was a
new female artist named Taylor Swift.

Chapter Twelve: One More Day In Heaven

Just as I had predicted, our single fell off the charts within the next couple of weeks. We tried to release another song called "We're Makin' Up," and it peaked at 54 on the charts. We even tried for a third time with "Easy Does It," and it pretty much did the same thing.

The band was in a bad place. We started second guessing every move we made. We even got to the point of firing Sparky because we felt he was unhappy with how we paid him. It seemed that Sparky had grown tired of the band and seemed overly concerned about how much money he was making. Looking back now I can't blame him. He had every right to be worried. The band and everything around us was falling down like Jenga blocks.

We tried replacing Sparky with Kevin Ray for a while, but it just wasn't the same. Kevin was a gifted guitarist and could sing really well, but the chemistry wasn't exactly right. We also gave Brian Nutter a shot. Same thing...incredible player but just didn't have the same mojo as Sparky did.

Everyone was so frustrated when DreamWorks announced that they were going to close up shop. James told us they were going to merge with Universal so we'd still have a record deal. For a moment we thought maybe the new label would save us. Maybe they'd get us where we wanted to go.

After meeting with the head of the label, Luke Lewis, I knew it was only a matter of time before he'd drop us too. He didn't understand the music at all. He responded to me in a meeting one time with, "Quit tryin' to reinvent the wheel...this is the music business." I knew right then we weren't on the same page.

Chapter Twelve: One More Day In Heaven

Despite how I felt about everything, we started making a new record. I had written a few songs for it but no one seemed to like the songs I turned in that much. Richard was at the helm and he wanted us to be more commercial. I tried my very best to stay focused but felt like it was all a big waste of time.

Our new label didn't seem that interested in what we were doing even though they said they were. We got Tom Buchavac and Brent Mason to come in and record with us to fill Sparky's shoes. Again, both of those guys are as pro as they come but it just wasn't the same.

After finishing up the record I felt numb. I didn't like it. I felt alone too. Richard, Keith and Trey seemed to dig it but I felt like it wasn't unique enough. Yes, there were cool moments and some good songs but it didn't sound like Hot Apple Pie. It sounded like any other Nashville record.

Not long after we turned in the record, the label dropped us. They said they had some other priorities they had to concentrate on and wished us luck. I was tired. I was sick of trying to please everyone else. I had started the HAP project because I felt we could make a difference and put out some new music that would impact people. Unfortunately, that didn't happen the way I wanted it to.

While I had been dealing with all the HAP drama Lisa and I had started The Franklin Bridal Ball. It was mostly Lisa though. I did whatever I could and helped fund it. She teamed up with two other talented business women to put on an event where we'd rent out several large rooms in a place called The Factory at Franklin.

We then rented 10'x10' booths to local wedding vendors so they could show off their wares to those getting married.

It was quite an ordeal. There was a fashion show, giveaways, food tastings and even limousines parked outside for couples to consider for their big day. Caterers, tent rental companies, bridal gown shops and anything else that went along with having a wedding were there. Lisa stayed very busy throughout the year getting ready for it.

I remember getting a call from Mom one day and she sounded upset. I could tell something was wrong immediately. She said, "Hello honey, you doin' ok?" I said, "What's wrong Mom?" She continued, "Honey I didn't know whether or not to call you but your Dad's in the hospital." She told me that he had been at McDonald's that morning for a sausage biscuit and then came home. Not long after she said he bent over in extreme pain and told her to call 911.

Everything she said after that was fuzzy. I told her I'd come home immediately. I called Lisa to tell her what had happened and told her to get her things together because we needed to head to Fairfield. At the time we had a little Mini Cooper car and we threw our bags in as fast as we could and headed North.

I sped the whole way. Normally it would take me about five and a half hours to get home. This time I was in Cincinnati in four and a half. I would've made even better time if I hadn't been pulled over by a cop in Covington, Kentucky. He clocked me going over one hundred miles per hour.

I told him the situation but he had no sympathy whatsoever. In fact, I'm pretty sure he moved extra slow in writing me up a 250-dollar ticket. I was so mad! But I continued on and drove straight to the Mercy Hospital in Fairfield. Mom had called me and said he was in ICU.

She told me that the doctor said it was pancreatitis. Evidently Dad had a gall bladder stone that was blocking his bile duct. It was a very painful but manageable condition. I was thankful, but still very worried. I met Mom at the hospital and went in to see him. They had him pretty drugged up, but he was coherent. He was happy to see me and smiled when I walked in.

He told me he had been in a lot of pain but it got a little better once they gave him some pain medicine. Mom asked me on the way to the hospital if she should call his other kids and let them know his condition. I didn't hesitate and said, "Absolutely. They need to know."

We hadn't been at the hospital very long before my brothers, Terry and Dinky arrived from Kentucky. They drove up together to check on Dad. As soon as they arrived, we all went in to see him. He was so thrilled to have us there. In fact, I remember him saying that evening, "This is the happiest day of my life to have all my boys in the same room together."

I spent a little more time with him that night and he told me that he loved me. He was doing pretty good and he said he thought he'd be fine. The doctors and nurses said it would be okay for us to go home and get some sleep that night. They were going to give Dad some antibiotics and possibly operate in the next day or so.

We said our goodbyes and headed to Mom and Dad's house. It was late in the night when we got a call from the hospital saying that Dad was not doing well and that we should come back to the hospital immediately. We didn't understand what was happening but we rushed back to check on him.

When we got there the staff told us that he "coded" during the night. They explained that coded meant that Dad had a cardiopulmonary arrest. Basically, he died and they had to resuscitate him. I was in shock and so was everybody else. We had no idea his situation was as bad as it was. When we left, Dad was okay and resting well. The doctors had it all under control.

To this day I'm not sure what happened. No matter how many questions I asked, the staff were vague about why he stopped breathing during the night. Maybe it was too much medication, maybe the nurses weren't checking on him...who knows.

The issue now was that he wasn't responding. He was breathing but he was in a coma. I'd talk to him but he never reacted at all. Of course, we called all of the family to let them know what happened. Everyone was just as surprised as we were. Even though pancreatitis is a serious condition it was normally a fixable one. Not very many people die from it. As long as a person gets the proper care, they go on to live normal lives.

For the next two weeks we waited, we cried, we prayed. I remember going into the restroom one day and crying harder than I ever have. It felt like I had been stabbed in the heart. I was so distraught. I prayed earnestly for God to heal him and make everything okay again.

During that time, I tried to do some bargaining with God. When I would pray, I'd tell God if he healed Dad that I would do His work and be a better Christian. I even thought about making a Christian record and going down that path. I knew that Dad's only hope was God.

Family and friends were flowing in and out of the hospital every day. Dad had so many friends that cared about him. Mom was a wreck in the waiting room. She wandered around from person to person thanking them for coming. She had a far off look in her eye and I was constantly making sure she was okay. I was scared for her. How was she going to live here in Ohio without Dad if something happened to him? Would I need to move her down to Tennessee? It was all too much at times.

One night in bed, Lisa and I were having a serious conversation about things and out of the blue I brought up having a child. Up until that point I was on the fence about it. But after seeing Dad in the condition he was in I wanted a family of my own. I wanted to be able to carry on the Seals name. That's when Lisa and I decided to have a baby.

The next day Mom said that she'd like to go and look for a black dress in case something happened to Dad. It broke my heart but I knew deep down that she just might need one.

Mom and Lisa wanted to go into a lady's clothing store and I said I was going to go check out a bookstore across the street. I was getting ready to go into the bookstore when an African-American guy poked me on the shoulder and said, "Can I pray for you?" I almost teared up right then and there and said, "Yes you can."

He said a nice thoughtful prayer and he asked the Lord out loud to comfort me. When he was done, he said, "Do you mind if we go inside and talk for a moment?" Of course, I agreed and we walked in and sat down at a table. He asked me if everything was alright with me and then I told him about Dad.

The concern in his eyes and gentle nature was comforting. I opened up to him that I had been praying non-stop for a week for Dad to be healed. He asked if we could pray again and I agreed. I couldn't help it, I cried listening to his words. When we finished I thanked him and we exchanged numbers. He said to call him anytime.

He also said, I have something else I want to talk to you about soon. He urged me to call him and we could talk about it the next time we met. He even said, "I feel God is telling me to tell you he has something special planned for you." It sparked my interest and I told him that I would call and we'd meet up soon.

When I left and met back up with Mom and Lisa, I told them all about my encounter. They were both as amazed as I was. We all wondered what "the something special" meant. I told them that it felt like God sent an angel that day to pray for me. For the first time in a week I felt hopeful that Dad just might survive this ordeal.

When I returned to the hospital Dad was worse. The doctor wanted to have a meeting with me. He said they had done an EEG and it wasn't good. An EEG is a monitoring method to record the electrical activity in Dad's brain. They basically said he was brain dead and there was no reason to continue his breathing and feeding tubes.

I was faced with the task of telling Mom that Dad was going to die. I don't know how, but I kept it together enough to tell her the news. She took it as well as she could and we wept. After talking with my brothers and sister and Dad's brother and sisters, I gave the doctors permission to pull his life support.

It was the hardest decision I ever made. I was a nervous wreck. All of my anxieties and depression came rolling back. I felt a void that I had never felt before. I couldn't see past the minute. The only thing I held on to was Mom, Lisa and God.

In fact, I called that stranger up that I had met at the bookstore. I told him Dad's prognosis. He prayed again for me over the phone and asked if I'd meet him for a cup of coffee the next day. We agreed to meet at the same place again.

When I got there, I felt completely out of it. I hadn't slept well and I was losing weight because of the stress. We sat down and he pulled a folder from his backpack. He told me that God had told him that I needed a new direction in my life that would help me get over the grief. He proceeded to give me a pitch to be a salesman for Amway.

To say that I was disappointed would be the understatement of my lifetime. I was so incredibly mad that I didn't even know how to react. I just kindly said, "I need to go" and got up and walked out. I didn't wait for his response, I didn't have any second thoughts, I just left the store and walked to my car.

The angel that I thought I'd been talking to turned out to be the devil. I looked straight into his eyes. To think he'd mess with my emotions and make a sales pitch during the death of my father was unfathomable. I had just been the victim of the worst kind of manipulation.

I tried my best to put it behind me. I had more pressing issues to deal with. I had to prepare for Dad's funeral and all the other things that come along with someone leaving this world. I needed to make sure Mom was not going to break down. She didn't know what she was going to do and I didn't either. We were all lost without Dad.

For about a week or so we were in and out of the hospital. There were several family members there every day. It was horrible to sit and watch my father basically starve to death. His heart was still beating, but his mind had checked out. His body was slowly fading away.

On the day he died I had just left his room to go home and get Mom and Lisa. Mom had told me to go through his bedroom drawer to see if there was anything that I'd like to have. His wallet was there. His wrist watches. His pocket knives. Little trinkets that he had kept over the years. In his wallet I found a picture of me when I was a little boy in the first credit card sleeve. I cried. That's when I heard the phone ring.

Mom came into the room and said, "We need to go on up to the hospital". I knew without her saying another word that he was gone. I went to visit him one last time in his hospital room. When I got there my sister Debbie was sitting there. When I looked at Dad, he didn't look like himself. His mouth was open and his face looked like a skeleton. The thing I noticed most though was his spirit was gone. I could no longer feel his presence in the room.

I knew at that very moment that God and heaven was absolutely real.

We buried Dad at Rose Hill Cemetery in Hamilton, Ohio July 25th, 2007. He was 79. Only a month or so before his 80th birthday. The family couldn't believe how many people came to his funeral and burial. It was standing room only. The man was so loved and will be missed by many.

I stayed for another couple of weeks with Mom. Lisa went back and forth once or twice during that time to tend to the Bridal Ball. I tried to help Mom wrap up loose ends with Dad's paperwork. I helped her around the house to fix a few things and just tried to be there for her. Lisa and I let Mom know that she could come home with us for a while.

She took us up on our offer and she came with us. She had a friend take her back to Ohio several weeks later. We discussed her moving down to Franklin but she didn't want to leave her friends and family in Fairfield. She said her sister Tootie wouldn't know what to do with herself if she did that. Mom assured me she was going to be okay.

I didn't pick up an instrument the whole time Dad was sick. I didn't have the desire. In fact, I got a call one day from a lady while dealing with Dad's arrangements. She was the casting director for a show called "The Million Dollar Quartet". It was a musical show based upon the 1956 Sun Record Studios impromptu jam session of Elvis Presley, Jerry Lee Lewis, Carl Perkins and Johnny Cash. She asked if I'd be interested in playing the part of The Killer. I kindly had to tell her no. My head was just too foggy to even consider it.

I did however write a song with my friend and co-writer Tommy Barnes about a month after Dad had passed. It was called, "One More Day In Heaven."

One More Day In Heaven

One day we're born, one day we die
People will mourn and people will cry
And people will miss them
to have and to hold
But He is the master and He's got a plan
Now don't you worry we're all in good hands
But when you love somebody it's still hard to let go

But one less day on earth
is one more day in heaven
They're dancin' with the angels
on a golden distant shore
You can think of it as a curse
but I look at it as a blessin'
One less day on earth
is one more day in heaven

When my father left
I was there by his side
He didn't say it
but I could see in his eyes
He felt comfort in knowin'
that he wasn't alone
There was somebody with him
to show him the way

Through the valley of darkness
to an uncloudy day
To where he's been livin'
to where he belongs

One less day on earth
is one more day in heaven
He's dancin' with the angels
on a golden distant shore
You can think of it as a curse
but I look at it as a blessin'
One less day on earth
is one more day in heaven

You can think of it as a curse
but I look at it as a blessin'
Yeah one less day on earth
is one more day in heaven

Words and Music by Tommy Barnes and Brady Seals

I grieved hard after my dad passed. I didn't want the world to keep spinning, for everyone to just go on with their lives like it never happened. I went back into a deep depression and was angry at God. I felt He had let me down. He had a great opportunity to heal my dad and send me down a musical path that would be focused on Christian music. I know now that was selfish and egotistical on my part, but it's how I felt at the time.

By the winter of '07 I wasn't feeling good at all. I was back to being anxious and depressed and knew I needed medication. I knew if I didn't head it off at the pass that I could sink even lower. And to add to my issues I started having trouble with my prostate.

At first, I just thought I was getting up a lot at night to go to the restroom but it started to disrupt my sleep. After a while it was happening during the daytime as well. Something was wrong. I could feel something deep in my body wasn't right. Sometimes it would hurt to urinate.

I went to visit a urologist and he diagnosed me with an enlarged prostate. He said that I might have a condition called acute prostatitis. I couldn't quite believe what I was hearing. There's no way my luck could be that bad. I just lost my father and now I had some sort of long-term medical condition?

The doctor put me on some medicine but I was still having issues. In fact, one day I remember my groin was hurting unusually bad. When I felt down there, I discovered a little bump that I had never felt before. I immediately thought I had prostate cancer. I had a full out breakdown.

Lisa was in a meeting with her girlfriends that day at the house. So, when I had the breakdown, I was alone in the bedroom. I certainly didn't want to come out weeping and complaining of my scrotum hurting and saying that I had cancer.

I spent an hour or so thinking the worst and mentally trying to prepare myself for the official diagnosis. I called the doctor's office and made an emergency appointment but it was still going to be a week before I could see him. I was a basket case.

When I was finally able to see him, he informed me that it was only a swollen blood vessel. It was nothing to worry about and the doctor sent me on my way. I came out of the doctor's office with a new lease on life. I still had a prostate issue but at least I didn't have cancer.

Several months later Lisa told me she was pregnant. At the time I was on medication for my prostate and had read that while on the drug it was next to impossible to be fertile. But I was. God really wanted us to have a child. It went from the saddest time of my life to the happiest time of my life within a matter of months.

I was going to be a dad. The thought was exciting and terrifying. I had so many emotions going on at the same time it was hard to concentrate. Overall, I was happy even though I was sad that our child would never be able to meet their grandad. He or she would never spend time with him and hear all his tall tales.

Never Barter With God

God is omniscient. He knew that I was going to have a baby before Dad got sick. He knew that my dark days would eventually turn to light. He knew my baby's name before I did. It says in the Bible in Jeremiah 1:5 KJV: *"Before I formed thee in the belly I knew thee; and before thou camest forth out of the womb I sanctified thee, [and] I ordained thee a prophet unto the nations."* I know He knew. I also know now that if it hadn't been for Dad's death my child would've most likely never been born.

The other thing to take away from this chapter is, never barter with God. He doesn't lack or need anything. God's very own existence comes from Himself, so He is not dependent on anyone or anything else.

We're dependent on Him. *"And he is before all things, and by him all things consist."* -Col 1:17 KJV. God needs nothing. *"God that made the world and all things therein, seeing that he is Lord of heaven and earth, dwelleth not in temples made with hands; Neither is worshipped with men's hands, as though he needed any thing, seeing he giveth to all life, and breath, and all things;"* -Acts 17: 24-25 KJV

I was desperate and selfish when Dad died. I wanted to keep my father on this earth longer than God intended. Simple as that. I didn't want to believe at the time that my Dad wasn't made for this earth, his real home is in heaven. I was going to miss him. I was scared that I couldn't live life without him, but God showed me the hard way that I could. He knew best.

CHAPTER THIRTEEN:
STARCITY

*"Thou art my hiding place; thou shalt preserve me from trouble;
thou shalt compass me about with songs of deliverance. Selah."*
-Psalm 32:7 KJV

My son Evan James Seals was born on September 15, 2008 in Franklin, Tennessee. We gave him the same middle name as my Dad's name, James. I liked the name Evan because it rhymes with heaven. God had given us a healthy beautiful boy.

For months leading up to his birth we were very worried though. Lisa and I had waited late in life to have a baby and we knew the older Lisa was the more dangerous it was for Evan's health. We trusted that God would handle it though, and we put it in His hands.

The doctors at Vanderbilt told us that he may be born with Down Syndrome. We had several ultrasounds done to check our little boy's progress. One particular procedure made us very anxious. It's called Amniocentesis. It's where a sample of the amniotic fluid surrounding the fetus is withdrawn through a needle inserted into the mother's uterus.

Thankfully the tests came back negative. After getting the news he was alright, Lisa and I sat in the car at the doctor's office and cried for thirty minutes. We were so relieved that he wasn't harmed during the test. We thanked God for answering our prayers. To this day I've never taken Evan's presence on this earth for granted. He's been God's greatest gift and my proudest accomplishment.

Evan was born at the Williamson County Hospital in Franklin. Lisa had to have a cesarean section because Evan's umbilical cord was wrapped around his upper body. The procedure went perfectly though. Lisa's doctor, Kim Scott, handed him to the nurse and she brought him over to a heated table. That was the first time I was able to get a close look at him. He was crying, but when I said, "Hey Evan, it's your dad", he became still and looked towards me. It was unforgettable.

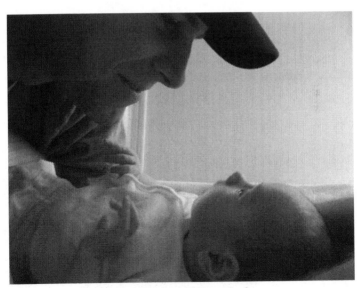

Brady Seals and Evan Seals
Photo Credit: Lisa Stewart

Hiking at Radnor Lake in Nashville, TN
Brady Seals and Evan Seals
Photo Credit: Lisa Stewart

We brought him back to the house after several days. I spent the next few months at home with Lisa and Evan. I couldn't believe I was now a dad. I realized what that meant pretty quickly though, having to get up and down through the night to make sure he wasn't suffocating under a blanket or something. Lisa seemed to love her new role as a mother, and she was wonderful with him.

When things settled down a little bit, we were able to travel to Ohio and Mississippi so the rest of the family could see our son. Mom was so excited and so was my Aunt Tootie. They treated him like a newborn king. It was good to see Mom happy again. It had been a very rough and lonely year for her without Dad.

I knew I needed to get back to work to pay for all the bills that were racking up. Hot Apple Pie tried to reinvent ourselves over and over but it just didn't work out. Trey had gotten to the point of wanting to go back to Louisiana and we couldn't blame him. We even tried to get Stan Lynch to come in and jam with me, Kevin Ray and Keith Horne, to see if there might be some magic. It sounded great, but Stan said he didn't know if he had the time to tour. He loved the idea of making a record though.

16 Ton Recording Studio- Nashville, TN
From left to right: Stan Lynch, Kevin Ray and Brady Seals

We finally came to the realization we had run our course as a band. We only had a few shows booked that we were obligated to play. After those dates, we decided to go our separate ways as friends. We gave it our all, but for some reason God didn't want us to move forward with it. I can say with certainty that God was watching out for me during Dad's cross over. It would have been extremely difficult to go through all that with tour dates looming over my head. I would've had to cancel several months of shows and would possibly have been sued because of it.

Dad had asked me in the hospital room to keep on making music and so I did. I was back into the routine of writing and recording. Stan and I had become good friends and he also urged me to keep doing what I was doing and said that somehow down the line it'd pay off.

My friend Joe Chambers invited me down to see a new project that he had been working on called the Musicians Hall of Fame Museum. I knew Joe because he also owned Chambers Guitars. He had three guitar stores scattered around the area and I did some part time work with him back in 2003 at his Cool Springs store in Franklin. It was five minutes from my house and it was therapeutic for me to just clock in and do my job. Most of the time it was just me and Ryan Wariner (Steve Wariner's son) sitting around playing music and talking about rock and roll. I cleaned instruments, checked people out at the cash register and helped sell guitars to Joe's customers.

While working at the Cool Springs store Joe shared his vision of starting the museum. It took him years to make it happen, but he did. He and his wife Linda worked feverishly to find a building, do all of the renovations and then track down all kinds of historical items to showcase to visitors.

I was thoroughly impressed when I was finally able to walk through the museum. They did an incredible job. The place looked fabulous! While on the tour, Joe showed me another large area that was going to be for guitar teachers to come in and give lessons to students. Immediately I thought it'd be a great spot for me to have a small studio and a place to work and write. I knew I needed a place other than the house since Evan had arrived. I didn't want to disturb him and Lisa. Joe loved the idea and we worked out a lease agreement and I moved in within a week and I set up my gear.

I spent the majority of my time at my studio space writing and recording. But I also had time to play a few shows with two artist friends of mine, Aaron Benward of the country duo Blue County and Brian McComas. We played some festivals using the same band and played the hits that we all had. We formed a little alliance and started to get a few shows as a trio.

I was also working with some other friends of mine, Brian and Nancy Eckert. They were helping me manage my career. I was producing other acts and working on my own projects, so having them in my corner really helped with everything I was doing. I just loved them as people. They were sincere and honest.

Nancy was an incredible music attorney and Brian was a great bass player and writer. They also owned a small studio in Germantown called Verge Recording. When I talked about cutting demos, they introduced me to their in-house studio engineer, Greg Strizek. I could tell he knew what he was doing after we chatted that day. I had him mix a few tracks and was floored by what he did. I knew we'd go on to become long-time friends and work together in the future.

One day, while standing in line at the movies, Lisa struck up a conversation with a step father and daughter waiting behind her. They got onto the subject of music somehow. They told Lisa that the girl was a singer and was trying to jump start her career. Lisa told them about me, Nancy and Brian and how I was a producer and the team could possibly help.

We met up weeks later and I heard her sing and felt like she could really do something in the biz. Her name was Amie Zimmerman but she wanted to go by Nikki Z. She was a pretty girl too and seemed to have it together for a teenager. We gathered some songs for her. Some were mine and others I collected from publisher friends. We recorded a few songs with some of the guys that would go on to become Jason Aldean's band.

The project fizzled out months later because Amie told us she was moving to LA to be with her real dad. It cost Nancy, Brian and me a lot of time and effort. We had just lined up a meeting with Scott Hendricks at Warner Brothers for him to hear her. Scott was impressed and requested a showcase. Unfortunately, we had to tell him about the situation that had arisen. It had put a bad taste in my mouth about producing, but undeterred I told myself it was probably just a one-off thing.

Around that same time, I met with a guy named David Bradley. He had been looking for a producer and someone to mentor him through the maze of madness of Nashville. Not only would I go on to produce his record, but I also helped him prepare for playing live and doing interviews. Lisa and I invited him over to the house to teach him a few tricks of the trade when he was on camera.

David came from England and was a huge country fan. He had a strong voice, a good look, and I thought he had a great story. I devoted the next several months to producing his record and to this day, I think it turned out to be a great sounding CD.

I worked on a few other projects as well. One was a Canadian country artist named Larry Berrio. I co-produced that CD with Gil Grand, another Northerner. The other artist was a kid from West Chester, Ohio named Coy Taylor. I enjoyed the process of working in the studio and being around great musicians and engineers.

While all this was going on, I recorded some demos of my own songs with my friends and fellow musicians Buddy and Jim Hyatt. They had a crew of stellar players that would charge a flat rate to record the main tracks for demos for songwriters in Nashville. I planned to record as many songs as I could afford, so I could begin looking for a new publishing deal.

Somewhere in the middle of all this activity I talked with Tracy Brown, the head of an independent radio promotion company called CO5. I figured that I could possibly work for them as a radio rep. I needed to bring in some money and getting into the record business side of things sounded fun.

In our conversations, she told me about a small independent record company called StarCity Recording. She suggested that I talk to them to see if they'd be interested in signing me as a recording artist. She said she'd give them a call for me. I was so appreciative but I was really hoping she'd give me a job.

Some days later, I received a call from a guy named Jeff Glixman, head of StarCity Recording. Tracy had called Jeff and shared my info and story with him. He asked if I'd send him some songs and, of course, I agreed.

I'd eventually find out that Jeff was the guy who produced Kansas back in the day. He also produced other rock acts such as Gary Moore, Yngwie Malmsteen, The Georgia Satellites and Black Sabbath. I was a huge fan of Kansas and The Georgia Satellites and thought this might be a perfect musical fit.

I can't remember how I sent my songs to him. Either through the mail or email. I had been used to sending people my songs and never hearing back. Nashville was notorious for doing that. But this time it was different. Jeff called me immediately and was extremely interested. He said he'd like to fly in to Nashville to meet me and he was bringing Phil Ehart, the drummer for Kansas, with him. He said if we can make this happen, Phil would be my manager.

I couldn't believe it all happened so quickly. The next thing I knew I was meeting at a J. Alexander's restaurant in downtown Nashville to talk about signing a record deal. Jeff and Phil were super nice and very excited about the possibility of me being on the label. After the meeting and some small talk Jeff asked me, "How can we make your dreams come true?"

Boy that was a loaded question. I told him that I'd like to release some songs to radio again and make a good living to support my family. He didn't bat an eye. He said he loved what he heard and wanted to get the ball rolling.

He explained that StarCity was a small company out of Pennsylvania. They were based out of a studio there called StarCity Recording Company and they had an investor that was ready to lay some big money down on a few new select artists. He went on to say their company was all about being creative and letting the artist be an artist. He didn't want to change a thing about me.

I told Lisa, when I got home from the meeting, that it went as well as a meeting could go. We were both thankful that things were getting ready to take off again.

Signing the record deal with StarCity
From left to right: Lisa Stewart, Evan Seals and Brady Seals
Photo Credit: Nancy Eckert

I called Brian and Nancy and told them about the meeting. I also had to tell Aaron and Brian that I needed to back off from pursuing more road gigs with them. They were all very happy for me and knew this might be a really good opportunity. Since we had all been working a little bit together, I wanted them to understand what had been offered to me, and get their blessing. They were all for it.

After the shock wore off, I got to work. I wanted to make sure I had some great songs for the CD. I had been writing with some great writers like Stan Lynch, my cousin TJ, Bobby Terry, Greg Friia, David Bradley and Richard Marx. The whole CD was supposed to be fun and upbeat. I co-wrote one song with David Bradley and Greg Friia, "Eeny Meny Miny Moe" at my house with Evan sitting in his baby carrier. I guess you could say he was a co-writer.

I had also been writing with an old radio DJ friend from Cincinnati, Bill Whyte. He and I got together one day and wrote a song called "Been There, Drunk That." It was a fun up-tempo song that I thought would be a perfect fit for the CD. After writing it, I knew the CD was complete.

Even though I was not a drinker, I had been around plenty in my line of work to know every little thing about it. When Jeff heard the song, he loved it. He felt like it should be a single. We planned a video, and began preparations to go out on the road. StarCity hired Nine North Records to be our radio promotion team. I had reservations about it simply because I had been talking with CO5 and Tracy was responsible for putting us all together in the first place.

In the end there wasn't much I could do about it, except give my opinion. The label had already made their decision. I felt terrible telling Tracy and my old friend David Newmark who worked with CO5 that StarCity had chosen to use another team.

The first single they released was a funny little song that TJ and I wrote called, "Ho Down". It didn't get any traction whatsoever with radio. And that was probably due to the lyrics. It was about a bar tramp that gets punched and knocked down on the dance floor by a jealous wife.

We followed it up with "Been There, Drunk That". We made a cool video and released it to radio. Nothing. It didn't even chart. The radio promotion team did not deliver on their promises. I was very disappointed in their company. I believe to this day that StarCity wasted money hiring them.

Here's how it works. A record label, investor or an individual pays Nine North a sum of money to promote their song(s) to radio. Nine North tells the artist and their team that they can't guarantee anything but they'll try their best to get the song(s) played. They in turn are supposed to call radio stations around the country and let the stations know they represent the artist in question and would ask the stations to consider playing the new single.

The fee that the label, investor or individual puts down also pays for flying the artist and an independent promotions guy/girl around the country to visit radio stations. Sometimes you play a few songs to the staff, sometimes you do an on-air interview or sometimes you do a free show for the station. It's called a listener appreciation show.

Nine North only had a handful of stations that would have independent artists like myself come in to talk about their projects. Most stations only play major label artists. So even though it seemed at the time that I was busy promoting the new single, there were only a few stations playing it in light rotation. I can't speak about any other genre of music but country, but independent radio promotion rarely works.

I toured the country playing shows and had a blast doing it. I had a few other artists opening for me. The English artist I produced, David Bradley and another label mate, Nathan Lee Jackson. Nathan brought his guitarist Keith Ridenour to accompany him. My band and crew were made up of some great people and stellar musicians.

Backstage during the Playtime Tour
From left to right (Front Row): Spencer "Spanky Dynamite" Bassett, Jamie O'Neal and Brady Seals

Not only did we play some cool venues and meet some great people but we were able to play tourists and visit some wonderful places. We visited Mount Rushmore and The Grand Canyon. We hiked mountains in Park City, Utah and in Bozeman, Montana. I remember climbing a mountain with Steve Cochran, John "Peepers" Calzavara and David Bradley on my 40th birthday.

Then one day, Jeff Glixman called to tell me that the label was in trouble financially. Jim Gentile was our main investor and evidently, he was taking a beating in the stock market. The Great Recession of 2008 was draining his accounts dry. Jeff told me everything needed to be suspended until further notice.

It didn't take very long until we realized that Jim was almost broke. It was now 2009 and "the dream" had become "a nightmare." The label was having to close down because of the lack of financing. There was really nothing I could do about it but start looking for another job.

I wasn't too heartbroken over losing the record deal. I had been through it before. I knew that God had a plan. I just prayed for God's Will to be done because I knew that He knew best.

Jeff called me to apologize, as did Phil. They were both very disappointed that we wouldn't be able to continue to make music together. We were all in the same boat and it was sinking. We promised to stay in touch and went our separate ways.

Several years later in 2011, Jeff and I worked on another small project with Christine and Dave Boyd for

Victory Cruise Lines down in Florida. Bill Whyte and I wrote their theme song and Victory used it for a TV commercial. Spanky, my friend and guitarist, traveled to Florida for a day and filmed it. That was the last real musical project that I was involved in with Jeff.

Several major events happened in 2010. First, the album I produced for David Bradley was released. It featured Rodney Crowell on his breakout single and video, "Hard Time Movin' On" written by Rivers Rutherford. It was truly a great song and heartfelt performance. Sadly, it didn't do much because it was an independent release. David ran into the same issues that I did at country radio. Independent country artists have an exceptionally tough time trying to get airplay.

That was also the year that I had $55,000 worth of music gear ruined in the Nashville flood. On May 1st and 2nd of that year, torrential rains belted Tennessee, Kentucky, and Mississippi. More than 13 inches of rain caused the Cumberland River to rise 52 feet and spill over into Nashville and the surrounding areas. The Red Cross put the death toll at 24, and property damage was virtually incalculable.

I remember it raining on the 1st day like it was pouring out of a bucket. Local news warned people to stay at home because of flash floods. They also projected that the Cumberland river might overflow. Of course, I didn't listen to the warnings. I remember getting in my truck and taking a drive towards Franklin to see just how bad it was. I needed to check because the next day the band and I were supposed to leave on the bus to head west to play a series of shows.

All of my gear, and some of my band's equipment, was stored at a place downtown called Soundcheck, located on the lip of the Cumberland River. Soundcheck was the largest music rehearsal, instrument rental, cartage and storage facility in the Southeast.

I headed down Franklin Road but didn't get far. I remember seeing the backside of Harlinsdale Farm flooded by the Harpeth River. I couldn't believe my eyes. I had to turn around because the police had blocked the road.

When I got home, I called our road manager, Steve, to ask if he'd heard anything. I asked him if we should go get our gear before conditions got any worse. He said that it was already too late. His friend Ivan was freaking out too. Ivan had tried to drive into Nashville to get his PA that was stored at Soundcheck and wasn't able to because the road had been shut down.

All I could do was wait. Steve was frantic trying to find a bus that was south of town to come and get us. The bus companies north of town wouldn't be able to. I called all the band members and told them the situation. I told them that they'd have to find some backup gear for the trip because getting our gear at Soundcheck was not an option.

Somehow, we managed to scrounge up enough equipment to make the trip happen but everyone was very worried. Luckily, I lived on a hill and knew that Lisa and Evan would be safe. So, we headed out and hoped for the best.

In the following days we heard about the destruction. Soundcheck took the biggest punch of the flood.

Equipment owned by tenants such as Keith Urban, Vince Gill and Brad Paisley were ruined, along with equipment and instruments belonging to scores of Nashville's rank-and-file musicians. Damages reached well into the millions of dollars. After hearing the horror stories of people losing their lives and homes, I couldn't complain too much. Even though I had lost a lot, at least I still had my house and family. One of my crew members, Kris Tweedy almost lost his life. His home was ruined in the flood. Rescue boats barely got him and his family out alive.

About a month after the flood we were able to go get our gear. Most of it had to be thrown away. Only a few things were salvageable. To this day I'm thankful that I had insurance that covered about $22,000 of my losses. Also, a local organization MusiCares was generous enough to write everyone involved with the catastrophe a check for $1000. God bless them.

FEAR NOT

It was a furious squall. The waves broke over the boat threatening to capsize it. The men on the boat thought they were going to drown and they were moments from going down. Jesus slept, with no worries in the world. The crew panicked thinking all hope was lost. Jesus got up, rebuked the wind and said to the waves, "Quiet! Be still!" The wind died down and was soon completely calm. He said to His disciples, "Why are you so afraid? Do you still have no faith?" They were terrified and asked each other, "Who is this? Even the wind and the waves obey him!"

I always loved that Bible story when I was a kid. You can read it for yourself in Mark 4:34-41. I think you'll come to the same conclusion as me. There's always hope when you have Jesus.

I have almost lost hope several times trying to make a living playing music. I had pretty much given up thoughts of being a recording artist before StarCity came along. I thought my glory days had come and gone.

The music business is unpredictable and turbulent. Like Jesus' disciples, I've pushed the panic button a time or two when things got rough. I didn't have enough faith in Him to weather the storms. If I would've only known there was a blessing on the horizon (a record deal!) maybe I could've slept peacefully on the boat like my Savior did.

Where you find hopelessness, you'll often find fear. Fear can sometimes immobilize you and make you want to give up. There are discrepancies as to how many times God mentions, "Fear not" or "Don't be afraid" or "I will fear no evil" in the bible. I don't know the exact amount, but I do know He says it a lot. He's adamant about telling us not to fear and never lose hope.

"Yea, though I walk through the valley of the shadow of death, I will fear no evil: for thou art with me; thy rod and thy staff they comfort me." -Psalms 23:4 KJV

"God is our refuge and strength, an ever-present help in trouble. Therefore we will not fear, though the earth give way and the mountains fall into the heart of the sea, though its waters roar and foam and the mountains quake with their surging." -Psalm 46:1-3 NIV

Fear does not come from God; it comes from Satan. *"For God hath not given us the spirit of fear; but of power, and of love, and of a sound mind." -2 Timothy 1:7 KJV.* Don't let Satan rule your life and determine what you can and cannot do. Fight him with all your might and with God's Word, and let him know who's boss. Have faith that Jesus will not desert you. Wait out the wind and rain and know there will be a bright shining sun that will be breaking through the clouds sometime soon.

CHAPTER FOURTEEN:
TOGETHER FOREVER

"And God shall wipe away all tears from their eyes; and there shall be no more death, neither sorrow, nor crying, neither shall there be any more pain: for the former things are passed away."
-Revelation 21:4 KJV

My sweet aunt, Irene "Tootie" Pennington passed away from cancer the same year of the Nashville flood. It really took its toll on Mom because they were so close. Before Tootie got sick she'd come by mom's house every day and check on her. Tootie was mom's favorite sister even though they fussed at each other. When I was a child and through my adult years Tootie would always come over for the holidays. She always supported me and loved me like her own child. She loved Evan the same way. When she passed and we went to her apartment to clear out her things I found pictures of me and Evan all over her house.

Mom didn't make a big deal out of it while Tootie was sick but she had found out that the endometrial cancer that she had years before was back. She had surgery to remove a small malignant tumor in her uterus back then, and the doctor assured her that he thought he got it all.

But I guess that wasn't the case. Mom didn't want to worry everybody.

Now Mom was faced with having to get radiation to try to battle it. It worried me and my brother Greg. Mom acted like she was completely fine. She said she had plenty of friends that would take her to get the treatments. Greg offered to take her since he was only one town away, but she said she'd manage.

I had taken several years off from touring to be at home with Lisa and Evan and be able to go see Mom. Mom would also have some of her friends drive her down every now and then so she could stay with us.

Hamilton, Ohio
From left to right: Evan Seals, Brady Seals and Jackie Seals
Photo Credit: Lisa Stewart

While visiting her in Ohio she wanted me to go with her to see the doctor in Cincinnati. It was just the two of us, Lisa and Evan stayed at Mom's house. Evidently, the doctor had previously ordered some testing and Mom was getting the results that day. The doctor told her that the tumor was growing but it was still very small. He explained that it was nothing really to worry about but she'd need to have tests done regularly to make sure it wasn't growing too fast. He even said, "Jackie, at your age you'd more likely die of some other ailment than this tumor."

The results didn't sit well with me at all. I felt we should get a second opinion. My last experience with doctors in Cincinnati didn't go well and I didn't want to take that chance again. I asked Mom if she'd be okay if we saw some doctors in Tennessee to get their opinions about her cancer.

She agreed, and within several weeks she was staying with us in Franklin. I scheduled an appointment for her to see a surgeon at Vanderbilt Hospital that specializes in cancer surgery. She was supposed to be the best at what she did. The surgeon requested for the doctor in Cincinnati to send all of Mom's test results for her to review.

After she reviewed the tests, Mom and I had a meeting with her. The lady was kind and very to the point. She told Mom that she not only needed radiation but she needed chemotherapy immediately. The doctor in Cincinnati was completely wrong. The new doctor believed that it was a very serious situation. Mom and I both shed tears in the doctor's office. Our worst fear had come to life.

I discussed the gravity of Mom's condition with Lisa and we decided that it'd be best if Mom moved in for a while, until she went through chemo. There's no way I would've let mom go through fighting cancer alone in Fairfield. Mom was always there for me and I was going to be there for her.

Thankfully Mom agreed to move in with us. We took a trip to Fairfield to get everything she would need for a long stay and made sure her house was secure while she was away.

My brother Greg was a bundle of nerves. So were Mom's friends and other family members. It was a very stressful time for everyone involved. We loaded up all of Mom's essentials and headed back to Tennessee.

For the next several months Mom received chemotherapy at a cancer clinic just down the street from where we lived in Cool Springs. The faculty and staff were so professional and kind. Overall, Mom was so incredibly strong while having to sit there and have that stuff pumped into her veins. She also had to endure the radiation treatments that would make her nauseous. At times, the combination of the two was almost too much for her.

The doctor ordered some new X-rays after a couple of months of treatment and the results were horrifying. She said that the cancer not only grew but it had started to spread. I came apart at the seams. I was so anxious that I found it hard to function. Mom wasn't dealing with it too well either. She was getting sicker by the day.

The worst part for Mom was losing her hair. She was always such a beautiful lady and she didn't like anyone to see her that way. She'd wear bandanas on her head to hide the hair loss. While at home Mom was constantly sick to her stomach because of the chemo. She grew weaker and weaker.

The one positive thing that came out of Mom staying with us was that Evan was able to really get to know her better. On the days Mom felt good they'd have so much fun together. They had a game that they would play where they'd chase each other around the house. Mom would also sit and color in Evan's coloring books with him and tell him stories. She was so gentle with him and he'd smile from ear to ear when she was around.

Mom's doctor asked to have a private meeting with me one day and I had a terrible feeling about it. She told me that she felt Mom only had between six months and a year left. There was not much more she could do. My heart sank. I asked whether or not Mom should continue to have her treatments and she said that was up to us. She said it might extend her life a little, but it wouldn't cure her.

When I left the building, I felt numb. I didn't know what I was going to say to Mom. In fact, when I got home, I didn't say anything. I needed Lisa's opinion and think about how I was going to break the news to my sweet and beautiful mother.

I finally gathered enough strength to sit Mom down and tell her the news. After I told her what the doctor said, we both sobbed. I couldn't stand the thought of Mom having to deal with the pain of dying. I asked her if she wanted to continue the chemo and she said yes. She wanted to have as much time with us as possible. It broke my heart.

Her condition continued to deteriorate rapidly. I had to take her to the emergency room several times. Her pain had become a big issue and we had to get some heavy-duty pain medicine for her. The medication needed to be administered every four hours for it to work effectively. I remember setting my alarm clock to go in and help mom take her medicine.

She reached the point where I called my brother Greg for him to come down and visit. I didn't know how much longer she was going to be with us. The six months that the doctor gave us had turned into three months. And to add to the stress we found out that my cousin Sharon in Ohio was terminally sick. It was all just too much to take.

I would lay awake at night praying that God would give me peace and strength. I talked to Him in my mind like a friend. Lisa was so busy making sure Evan was taken care of that I didn't want to burden her with more than what she was already dealing with. God was the one I went to. He was my shelter.

Mom and I were able to discuss all of her wishes with me when the time came for her to cross over. She was able to sit with Greg and do the same thing. Even though it was extremely difficult to talk through the things that would need to be taken care of, it was a blessing to be able to do so.

Mom eventually got to the point of having Morphine on a drip. She was in extreme pain all the time. She told me that it was time for her to go to Hospice. She had endured all she could and she was ready to meet her maker. She didn't want to die in the house with Evan there.

The ambulance came to get her and I followed it downtown to a section of the hospital that's meant to keep people comfortable while they're dying. The staff was so helpful and sympathetic. I checked Mom in and they assigned her a room. I sat there alone and waited.

I remember thinking that it couldn't get any worse than this. I got to a place in my mind of wanting Mom to die because of the pain and suffering she was having to endure. I actually went up to her and whispered in her ear, "I love you Mom. It's okay to go."

The lady nurse told me it may take several days for her to pass and if I needed to go home and take care of anything it would be okay. I took her advice and headed back to the house to check on Lisa and Evan. I visited Mom three or four times and would sit in there for hours watching over her during the next couple of days. The one time that I wasn't at the hospital the nurse called me and said that mom had just passed away. She told me she was standing beside her when she breathed her final breath.

I had missed it once again. I wanted to be the one holding her hand while she crossed over to the other side. But for some reason Mom and Dad didn't want me to have to remember that. Maybe they were just in too much pain and just couldn't wait. Maybe it was just how God wanted it. I don't know, but it was hard on me. Very, very hard.

I know that Mom was happy when she saw Jesus, her mom and dad, my dad, her daughter Vanessa, her aunt Tressie, Tootie and the rest of her family at the gates of heaven. Oh what a reunion it must've been. She was one of the Godliest women that I've ever met and there's no question she got a Fast Pass ticket into The Promised Land. She died September 9th, 2012.

I'm not sure how I got through transporting Mom up to Ohio and for her funeral. Just like with Dad, there were so many people that attended. Mom didn't want an open casket. She had joked when she was alive and told me, "Close me up, I don't want anybody walkin' by me and lookin' at my old dead body."

When packing up her things at the house I found little sticky notes where she had labeled everything for me. In her handwriting she let me know who the item should go to. Bless her heart, she knew when she was writing those notes that her days were numbered. It made me smile and cry at the same time.

Several months after she passed, I put Dad and Mom's house on the market. I really didn't want to sell it, but I knew that I wouldn't be able to tend to it from Tennessee. I took photos of every room so I'd remember the last place I grew up. It sold after just a few days and I had to go back to Ohio and move all the furniture out. I gave most of it away to family and took the rest back to Franklin in a U-Haul truck. I couldn't believe it had come to that. Both of my parents and my childhood home were gone.

I Am Weak, He Is Strong

"But he said to me, 'My grace is sufficient for you, for my power is made perfect in weakness.' Therefore I will boast all the more gladly about my weaknesses, so that Christ's power may rest

on me. That is why, for Christ's sake, I delight in weaknesses, in insults, in hardships, in persecutions, in difficulties. For when I am weak, then I am strong." -2 Corinthians 12:9-10 NIV

If your life is like mine, there have been times when I felt drained and exhausted by grief. Life's responsibilities and burdens can literally bring you to your knees. We've all reached the point where we didn't know if we could take another step, right? I've laid in bed with depression. I've been physically ill but thankfully I'm healthy overall. Imagine having a terminal disease or a lifelong handicap. Life is hard!

And you know what? Our culture seems to have no pity on us. Weakness is looked down upon. Our world wants us to hide our emotions and not talk about our disabilities and mental illnesses. They don't want to hear about our "doom and gloom." And yet the Bible and particularly, apostle Paul, advocate Christians to brag about their weaknesses and shortcomings.

In 2 Corinthians 12:7-10 ESV, Paul describes the thorn in his flesh. It says, *"a thorn was given to me in the flesh, a messenger of Satan to harass me, to keep me from becoming conceited. Three times I pleaded with the Lord about this, that it should leave me. But he said to me, 'My grace is sufficient for you, for my power is made perfect in weakness.' Therefore I will boast all the more gladly of my weaknesses, so that the power of Christ may rest upon me. For the sake of Christ, then I am content with weaknesses, insults, hardships, persecutions, and calamities. For when I am weak, then I am strong."*

To boast? To brag? Woah...that's a shocker. Imagine if Nike's slogan was "Don't Do It, Let God Do It Instead". I don't think that'd fly.

God wants us out there talking about our weaknesses. Why? I believe it's because He wants people to know that He comes running when we need Him. You see, instead of God removing the difficult circumstance from Paul's life, He provided a way to overcome it through strengthening Paul. The Bible says "my power is made *perfect* in weakness." Because of God's perfect design, we can relax and know that God has everything under control. We can lean on Him when times get difficult. As 2 Corinthians 13:9 NIV says, *"We are glad whenever we are weak but you are strong; and our prayer is that you may be fully restored."*

CHAPTER FIFTEEN:
MUSIC CITY PICKERS

"The Lord shall command the blessing upon thee in thy
storehouses, and in all that thou settest thine hand unto; and he
shall bless thee in the land which the Lord thy God giveth thee."
-Deuteronomy 28:8 KJV

Several years before Mom died, I started selling off guitars that I didn't need any more on eBay. The first guitar I sold was a Rickenbacker and it sold within thirty minutes of listing it. I knew that I had made a mistake and priced it too low. It gave me a rush though. I realized that if I had more guitars, I could probably make a living selling them.

My friend Steve Cochran called me out of the blue one day and said that Ben Jumper, the guy that owned Soundcheck, the rehearsal facility downtown, was selling off a bunch of gear that had been damaged in the Nashville flood. Steve wanted to know if I wanted to go in half with him and buy the gear, clean it up and then sell it.

I agreed to meet him down there and see how badly damaged the gear was. Surprisingly it wasn't that bad. Only a few things were actually damaged. Steve and I bought the stuff and got to work creating an inventory list. I took pictures of everything and we created an eBay account and started selling each item. In the end we profited. A lot!

It seemed I had a knack for it, just like my grandpa did. He was known around Hamilton, Ohio to be a good barterer. I had always been a gear head and knew a lot about the stuff we were selling. It seemed like a good way for me to make a living. I just needed products, a way to keep up with the items, and find out the best way to ship it all. If I could do that, I wouldn't have to tour. I could stay at home and be with my family. Eventually Steve pursued other businesses, so I continued alone with buying and selling.

I started buying gear off the online classified website, Craigslist. I'd offer a little lower than their asking price then turn around and sell it for market value. I started researching vintage guitars. I began with buying the book, George Gruhn's Guide to Vintage Guitars. I'd go page by page reading about the things that affected the value of the instrument. The book was published to be an essential aid for collectors, dealers and players. It provided specifications, serial numbers, and other pertinent information for determining the originality of vintage American acoustic and electric fretted instruments.

I made a lot of mistakes early on. I'd identify the guitar as a different model than what it really was or I'd determine the instrument was all original when in actuality it wasn't. I kept trying though. I'd go to every guitar show that came to town to learn, buy and sell.

When listing a Gibson Les Paul guitar online a guy named Gabe Hernandez contacted me to let me know my listing was inaccurate. He told me it was a different model than I described. When I looked further into it I realized he was right on some things, but wrong on others. I let him know I appreciated the information. We talked some and struck up a friendship.

That friendship turned into a partnership. We joined forces and put our money together to buy more and more gear. Not only guitars, but amplifiers, mandolins and banjos. We needed a name so I came up with the name Music City Pickers. I've always been a fan of the TV show American Pickers so I wanted to incorporate that into our store name. I thought it had a cool double meaning.

Music City Pickers Store
From left to right: Gabe Hernandez, Mike Wolfe (from American Pickers) and Brady Seals
Photo Credit: Kevin Schuck

Before we knew it, we had built up quite a stash of gear. I was good at finding and Gabe was good at selling. Gabe came up with the idea of traveling to different cities and buying musical instruments. He had worked for another guy years before that did that with baseball cards.

Our first city was West Chester, Ohio. I knew that I could get the word out around my hometown and have a lot of people show up with stuff to sell. Gabe and I had about $50,000 to work with, hoping to max out our investment money.

We'd set up in a hotel conference room with our banners propped up in the lobby directing visitors to our location. We'd buy ads in the local papers to let people know we were coming to their town to buy. We'd try to get as much publicity our dollars could afford. I'd even call local radio stations to let them know what we were up to.

To our surprise it worked! We'd usually buy around $25,000 worth of gear every time we made a trip. It worked really well for several of the cities but there were a few that weren't really worth the hassle of it all. We realized that if it hadn't been for one or two people who had brought a lot of gear, we probably would've lost money.

Gabe and I sold gear out of our garages for about a year until we decided to open a brick and mortar store. While searching for a place I told Gabe about a cool section of Nashville that I thought would be perfect for us. It was right off the infamous Music Row (16th Avenue). It was called Edgehill Village. It was a hip old warehouse that housed White Way Cleaners back in the 1930s. The new owners had just renovated the big plant and were leasing space there.

Gabe agreed after seeing the space. It had this urban industrial vibe that was perfect. I called a designer friend named Bobby McCloud to come in and help us design the inside. We wanted the customers to have a wow factor when visiting our store. We went in cahoots with another guy named Stephen "Elvis" Shutts who had a small shop called Rockology. He sold vintage rock and roll memorabilia and we thought it'd be an ideal match up.

Music City Pickers
Nashville, Tennessee Location

We decided we'd do just one more road trip and then try another tactic to find gear in the future. Our last buying show was Lexington, KY. I called a few friends of mine to let them know I was coming to their area and to let their musician friends know we'd be there. One friend was Randy Burchfield. He was the drummer for Josh Logan back in the day. We toured together for about a year in the '80s.

I remember getting a call from Randy saying that he knew a girl who owned Keith Whitley's guitar and was looking to sell it. I got excited knowing that I may be able to buy the country legend's guitar. I told him to tell her to come by and see us.

When she showed up, I saw the case she was carrying. It had Keith's autograph written in white marker on the top. After a closer look I noticed that it also had a baggage tag with Keith's name, address and phone number. It also appeared that it was authentic. When I took out the guitar it was a Martin Sigma SE-36 acoustic electric guitar. The guitar itself was a little rare but wasn't worth much on its own.

I told the girl that I'd need proof that it actually belonged to Keith because at that point the case was worth more than the guitar. She left a little disappointed but she said she'd try to find a way to prove it. Within an hour she called me back and told me to look up a YouTube link where Keith was playing it. Sure enough, it was his guitar.

I told her to come back to see us and I'd purchase it from her. When I offered her what I did, Gabe was very reluctant. He thought it was way too much money. I had to explain to him that Keith was an iconic figure in the country world. Gabe had no idea who he was because he was a rock guy.

We bought it and I was as proud as I could be. I called my publicist, Amy Willis at the time and told her the story. I asked if she'd put out a press release telling the world that we bought Keith's guitar. She thought it'd make a great story and within a day or so people everywhere knew about the guitar.

The day the press release went out I got a call from Amy saying that a country artist's manager called her and told her that her artist wanted to buy it. I told Amy that I was getting ready to list it on eBay and she'd have to come up with our minimum bid. She got off the phone and called me back within thirty minutes saying that the manager would come in that day and write us a check. I asked Amy who the artist was and she said the manager didn't want to say yet.

The person turned out to be an up and comer country artist named Chris Young. He had been a huge Keith Whitley fan and he didn't want the guitar to get away. The manager came in and bought it for Chris. He ended up playing it several months later when he sang a cover of Keith's classic song, "Don't Close Your Eyes" on The Grand Ole Opry.

The story goes that in the mid-to late '80s, Keith Whitley performed with mainly three guitars: A Fender Telecaster, a Martin acoustic, and a Sigma by Martin acoustic electric. Two of the guitars have been seen on display at a few museums in the southeast since Keith's passing. The Sigma by Martin, however, remained in the hands of a family friend and musician, Earl Watkins.

Earl previously owned the Circle H Saloon near Lexington, Kentucky. Keith and Earl became close friends and even played music together at the venue. During a visit to the Circle H Saloon in 1987, Keith traded his Sigma by Martin for a Fender Telecaster that belonged to one of Watkins' band mates, Jerry Fannin. Not long after that, Earl purchased Keith's guitar from Jerry for $500. Watkins would later pass it on to his daughter Jeanne, who would go on to sell it to us.

The grand opening of the shop was one to be remembered. Lisa helped with putting on an upscale event. We sent out formal invitations to all our friends to kick off our new venture. We catered in food and had bartenders serving cocktails throughout the night. The store looked amazing! The place was packed with Nashville artists that night.

I had set up a small PA in the corner where some of my friends could just walk up and plug in with an acoustic guitar and sing for everyone. Gabe and I got up and welcomed everyone and I asked my friend Gordon Kennedy to come up and play a few of his hits. The intimate acoustic setting was so special that evening that it sparked the idea of having weekly songwriter shows in the store.

I had also invited my ex-band mate, Tim Rushlow to come by and visit. I was thrilled when I saw him walk in. It had been years since we had seen one another. Several people asked if he and I would get up and perform together and we did. We sang three or four Little Texas songs and the crowd went wild. He and I stayed in communication after that night and worked out all of our differences. We remain good friends to this day.

With the shop being right off Music Row we had some incredible artists come by and visit. John Prine,

Rodney Crowell, Kacey Musgraves, Sam Pallidio, The Mavericks, Brothers Osborne and many others. Taylor Swift even shot a Keds photo ad in there because they liked the store's vibe so much.

The television show "Nashville" was hot and heavy during that time and they came in asking if we could rent some gear to them for the show. Of course, we said yes. We asked if it'd be possible to visit the show sometime and watch an episode being filmed. They were kind enough to let us do that and we met some of the cast and crew.

I stayed in business with Gabe for about a year or so, but I was ready to make a change. I wanted to stay in the music store business but I wanted to do it alone. There were several reasons that Gabe and I didn't see eye to eye but I wished him well. We split up the inventory and parted ways when our lease was up.

Gabe and I had hired a young guy that was working in the little pizza joint behind our shop named Kevin Schuck. At first, he was doing a lot of our shipping and cleaning the instruments. He was a hard worker and really had a lot of knowledge about gear since he was a guitarist himself.

When I decided to go off on my own, I kept the name Music City Pickers and asked Kevin if he wanted to move forward with me and he said he would. I told him that I'd like to make him the store manager and give him a commission when he found gear for us to sell. We moved into a little space at Soundcheck for our office and also had a spot in the warehouse in the back where we'd keep our inventory to ship out.

Almost all of our business was online. We'd sell on eBay and a new website that had just popped up called Reverb.com. Every now and then people would drop by the shop. Being there at Soundcheck, all the musicians were aware of us. We had Joe Bonamassa, John Oates and some other big-name artists stop in.

Life at home was good but Lisa and I were not seeing eye to eye on disciplining Evan. I thought she was too easy on him and she thought I was too hard on him. Evan was an amazing boy. He was so bright and kind. I couldn't have been prouder. We had enrolled him into Pre-K so he could get used to being around other kids and make some friends. In school he had some problems with respecting the personal space of other kids. He was also a little too rambunctious at times.

I recommended that Lisa and I go see a Christian counselor since we were arguing so much about it. I thought having a referee in the room would help us see things more objectively. We chose to see a lady at our church and she was wonderful. We were able to work through some of our problems and made the changes that she suggested.

I was still having some emotional issues from Mom and Tootie passing away. I got back on some anti-depressants so I wouldn't sink even lower. My whole childhood foundation was gone and it was hard on me. I kept on feeling like I was the next in line and the thought was scary. I was now 43 and I felt life was slipping away.

MCP (Music City Pickers) did pretty well for about a year at Soundcheck but the drive from Franklin to Nashville was grueling every day. Nashville was beginning to be a very popular place to live and visit. The TV show

Nashville really boosted people's attraction to the town and so did all of our sports teams. Big corporations were coming in and buying up real estate everywhere. It had got to the point where when you drove down some streets you couldn't see the sun because of all the high-rises. Traffic was terrible.

If we had been a business that relied on foot traffic we would've stayed where we were, but that wasn't the case. We were mainly an online business that shipped our products. I started looking for a place that was closer to Franklin.

Eventually I found a great space that was only five minutes from my house. It was approximately 2500 square feet and was perfect for what we needed. With the advice from my friend Joe Chambers I decided to buy the property instead of renting it. Joe told me it would pay off in the end.

Music City Pickers
Franklin, Tennessee Location

I don't think I could've done it without the money I received from Mom and Dad. After I sold their house, I was able to put a big down payment on the building. That helped tremendously with the financial strain.

I'd sit at home at night and draw up how I wanted the place to look and what kind of renovations would need to happen to make the space work for us. I hired a contractor to do most of the major renovations and Kevin and I did all the rest. Lisa helped a little but she was super busy with Evan. She was also doing more and more voice-over work and acting.

Once the renovations were done, Kevin and I along with some friends moved in. It felt amazing to have our own space. I had my own office that doubled as a writer's room and recording studio. We had a warehouse space for our gear, a photography room, lesson rooms, a break area, restrooms and a large showroom in the front.

We were buying instruments left and right. We'd try to find people that were getting rid of their collections and just buy all of it. Of course, we made a few mistakes here and there but overall, we were rockin' and rollin'.

I had several people working for me. One was Micah Tanner. He was much younger than me but was tenacious and had a lot of connections and was good at finding gear. In fact, he put me in touch with Peter Frampton. He said that Peter had some amplifiers he wanted to sell and we jumped on the opportunity.

My friend Gordon Kennedy was good friends with Peter as well so I called him to see if he could get us all together. The next thing I knew I was over at Peter's studio listening to some new music he and Gordon had been working on. Ironically enough the studio that we met in used to belong to Richard Landis. It was the same place where we recorded Hot Apple Pie's record that never came out.

Phenix Studios
From left to right: Gordon Kennedy, Brady Seals and Peter Frampton
Photo Credit: Steve Cochran

God had led me to a place in life that I thought I'd never be. I was the owner of my own business five minutes from my house. I bought my own business condo which had always been a goal of mine. I had a family at home waiting for me every night at closing time.

I was going to church a lot and had left all my burdens at the foot of the cross. As a family we started attending Fellowship Bible Church in Brentwood, TN and it was good for our souls. The preaching there by Dr. Michael Easley was incredible. He was more of a teacher than a preacher. Every Sunday Lisa and I would walk away with a new perspective on life. We began to grow as Christians and life seemed to be headed in the right direction.

Go Tell It On The Mountain

This was the time of my life where I was taught to witness from my pastor, Michael at Fellowship Bible Church. I wanted to go out and let everyone know about the glory of God. I was appalled with the sad truth that eighty-five percent of Christians never invite anyone to church, and 95 percent never win anyone to Christ. That was staggering for me. I wanted to do my part, even if it was in a small way.

I used social media to get the word out. Facebook and YouTube were my main outlets. I would go on walks in the morning and use a selfie stick and my phone to video myself talking about life, music or whatever I could think of at the time. I'd slip in a scripture now and then or something inspiring to lift people's spirits. I called it "Walkin' & Talkin'".

"So shall my word be that goeth forth out of my mouth: it shall not return unto me void, but it shall accomplish that which I please, and it shall prosper in the thing whereto I sent it."
-Isaiah 55:11 KJV

I think a lot of Christians don't witness because they feel they lack the knowledge of God's Word. The fear of losing friends also silences them. In many parts of the world, persecution is a real threat. Other times it's just a lack of conviction. I know that in the past I didn't witness because I didn't want to be a hypocrite. But none of these obstacles should keep us from spreading the hope, love and eternal promise God has given us.

Even if we just spread this one simple verse with non-believers... *"For God so loved the world that he gave his only begotten Son, that whoever believes in Him should not perish but have everlasting life." -John 3:16 NKJV*

Chapter Sixteen:
While My Guitar Gently Weeps

"The thief cometh not, but for to steal, and to kill, and to destroy: I am come that they might have life, and that they might have it more abundantly." -John 10:10 KJV

My favorite cousin and one of my mom's best friends, Sharon Carito, passed away in 2013. She'd been fighting Acute Myeloid Leukemia for quite some time and it finally took its toll on her body. We were all devastated.

I grew up hanging out with Sharon and her two daughters, Angie and Kristie. They were like sisters to me. I hated that they now had to deal with the kind of heartache I had just experienced. And to make matters worse, their father, Tom, would pass away the following year. It was all just too much to bear.

Life, as I once knew it, was changed forever. All of my immediate family were now in Heaven. There were times when I'd be alone and just break down and cry. The grief was heavy. I was never a drinker and long gone were the days of smoking pot. Prayer, my new family, work and antidepressant medication got me through.

Music had always been my helping hand, and I knew that it'd be good for me to listen, perform, write and record again. Right around that same time Porter called me to ask if I'd be interested in writing with him and a kid named Jackson Nance. He said Jackson was really young and talented and had some interest at Warner Bros.

I jumped at the chance. I knew I needed it. Even if just for the social aspect. I wanted to shake off some of the rust of sitting idle for so long. We met at the store one day when I knew that I wouldn't be swamped. It felt good to get back at it. I could feel the dreamer gears in my mind starting to run more smoothly.

The business had been doing pretty well for quite some time, but the tide was shifting. I had started selling gear with Steve in 2010, started MCP in 2011, went out on my own in 2012 and it was now 2014. I noticed several major changes that were affecting my financial bottom line.

The competition was starting to snag up all the local gear. My friend and guitarist Tom Buchavac now had a music consignment store in Berry Hill called 2nd Gear. My old partner Gabe had his store that was constantly searching for instruments to buy and the big boys like Guitar Center, Gruhn Guitars and Carter Vintage were always on the lookout for musical gear to flip.

But the biggest change was Reverb.com. When Reverb first came onto the scene it was a welcome change. Musicians and store owners had been at the mercy of eBay to sell their gear online. eBay's fees and guidelines seemed to be skewed towards the buyer instead of the seller.

Reverb had now changed that for everyone. I had been preaching for years that the music gear buying and selling business needed something like it. In fact, I even thought at one point of starting my own online outlet for musicians. I had gone as far as getting several friends involved, like Brian and Nancy Eckert and my neighborhood banker friend Brian O'Neil, to see if it was possible.

After several meetings and setting up a focus group asking musicians their wants and needs, we decided to throw in the towel. We would have needed to raise some major money to get it off the ground. It would have taken years and years and a whole lot of risk to make it happen. But that's exactly what Reverb did. In the end they raised 47 million dollars to launch.

Reverb had now made it easy for musicians to find what they wanted anywhere in the world and have it shipped to them. And Reverb made it incredibly easy to list your instrument and show the seller how to box it up and send it to their buyer. The other major thing that Reverb did was give everyone that visited the site, access to a buyer's guide. Now everyone knew what their gear was worth.

I knew in my heart that it was only a matter of time before we'd have to close up shop. The competition was too great. The veil of what everyone's gear was worth had now been lifted. There weren't any "deals" to be had anymore. I knew I needed to look for an exit plan.

Music. That's what I felt like I had been put on the planet to do. I wanted to figure out a way to get back into it, without having to go out on the road. I didn't want to leave Lisa and Evan at the house while I was off touring. I was not going to miss Evan's early childhood.

For the next two years I fought a losing battle. I tried and tried to work extra hard to find gear. Kevin was working non-stop to find product too, but there just wasn't enough to be had. We even tried doing more guitar and banjo lessons but that still couldn't keep us afloat. I met with business advisors to see if there was anything I could do to raise my profitability. I did everything I could to save the guitar shop but I knew deep down that I'd need to do something else to bring in more income for the family.

That's when I came up with the idea of Music City Pickers LIVE! I had been playing a few songwriter shows around town, and I thought I could possibly put on my own show. Gordon Kennedy and I had struck up a solid friendship and I thought he'd be perfect to team up with. One day out of the blue he said that he had just played a venue in Franklin called, The Little Brick Theater, and thought it might be a cool place for us to have our shows.

I was familiar with the theater because it was located in The Factory at Franklin where Lisa and I hosted The Franklin Bridal Ball. I went over one day to check it out and talked to a lady named Tammy to see about renting it for our shows. She loved the idea and wanted to help us any way she could.

Gordon and I started rounding up all of our songwriter friends to let them know what we were getting ready to do. I researched how to best sell tickets online and get the word out. We put our website and social media sites up and hired Nicole Witt at Brickshore Media to help us with a press release. We had several friends that so graciously volunteered to help out as well. We had our first show on November 3rd, 2016.

The lineup was incredible. Lisa hosted the night and introduced everyone to the stage. Gordon and I opened the show along with Larry Stewart from the band, Restless Heart and then had a brief intermission. Then Ricky Skaggs and his wife Sharon played a set with Gordon accompanying them. It was a huge success. The audience seemed to love it!

Little Brick Theater- Music City Pickers LIVE! Opening Show
From left to right: Brady Seals, Ricky Skaggs and Gordon Kennedy

We had invited a lot of press to the show and we received rave reviews the following days. We felt that we had hit gold. After that debut night we were confident that we could continue on with the concept and start doing weekly shows.

Some of the shows that followed were magical. Particularly when Rory Burke sang the song he co-wrote, "Most Beautiful Girl" for Charlie Rich. The audience was in awe hearing that classic from one of the men who wrote it. Another special songwriter moment is when Tommy Simms got up with Gordon and sang the song that they co-wrote, "Change The World" that Eric Clapton made famous. The songwriters that played our show were spectacular.

We had another epic moment happen when Gordon and his Beatles tribute band played at the theater. Peter Frampton got up and played "While My Guitar Gently Weeps." The crowd went absolutely berserk. I did too! I had always appreciated Peter throughout the years, but after hearing him play live, I became a fan.

Little Brick Theater- Music City Pickers LIVE! Opening Show
From left to right: Brady Seals, Larry Stewart and
Gordon Kennedy

Little Brick Theater- Music City Pickers LIVE!
From left to right: Brady Seals, Paul Jefferson, Porter Howell and
Sonny LeMaire

Lisa had been hosting the shows and would occasionally sing with Gordon and me. She was a songwriter as well, and she had co-written a song years before called "Sky Full of Angels," that had become the Southern Gospel Associations, Gospel Song of the Year in 2007. She seemed to really love putting on the shows each week and really helped get the word out and find sponsors for the event. When 2017 rolled around, I noticed a difference in our relationship. Something had changed, and I didn't quite know what it was. I felt she was upset with me somehow. She seemed uninterested when we talked. She also seemed to spend most of her time with Evan, even when I would come home from work.

We continued on, nonetheless. We had our morning ritual of having coffee together in the sunroom. We'd sit and watch the birds and discuss life in general. She never really said there was anything particular wrong though. She just seemed unsettled. I also noticed that she was starting to get frustrated more than usual anytime I would grumble about my aches or pains. She was really into health and fitness, essential oils and yoga and I thought she just felt I needed more of that in my life.

I thought our marriage was pretty solid though. We'd go visit her parents in Mississippi, go on little trips with Evan to Gatlinburg and have dinner at the table every night after I'd get home from work. Yeah, sometimes our days were mundane but I figured more exciting things were just around the bend. I just needed to get the income situation figured out.

I told Kevin that it was just a matter of time before the guitar shop was going to close. I advised him to start looking around to find another job. I didn't want to leave him high and dry. In fact, I probably stayed in business three or four months longer than I should've just to give him a job. I knew he had a wife and a new baby and I figured he needed the money.

One day while I was driving into work, I noticed that there was another business for sale two doors down from me. When I saw how much they were asking I was shocked. It was way more than I had imagined. I came home and told Lisa and we both agreed that it would be best to go ahead and sell.

I called a broker and before I had even put it on the market, I had someone interested. They made an offer that I couldn't refuse. They agreed for Kevin and I to rent the back warehouse from them for a year so we could continue to stay in business long enough to sell the rest of our inventory. It was going to be cramped but it was an ideal situation.

I accepted the offer. I had made more than enough profit from the building to cover any losses that I had from the business. I was so grateful even though I hated to have to sell. Kevin and I had thirty days to move all of the store merchandise and sell off anything that would be too much trouble to move.

When I told Lisa, I thought she would've been happier. I thought she would have seen that I would be able to spend more time at home now. I figured I'd just buy and sell instruments on the side and do a few road gigs here and there to pay for the bills. I thought wrong. She didn't hardly react at all. I'd soon find out why.

I truly don't want to go into details about the following months between Lisa and I. We have both discussed what happened with our son, in our own way and he doesn't need to read about his parent's marriage in this book. Essentially, our marriage failed and Lisa and I would divorce a couple of years later.

REJECTION & ABANDONMENT

I felt rejected after Lisa left. She no longer wanted to be married to me and it felt like a dagger to the heart. I didn't feel worthy, loved or accepted. I was lost and felt hopeless. My whole world had been turned upside down. I also knew that no matter how quick I'd bounce back the ripple effect of the divorce would last a lifetime.

I was familiar with the feeling of rejection. I had experienced a lot of it in my life. From not making the cut for a sports team to losing major record deals. None of them came close to the pain I felt during my separation with Lisa though. This pain was on another level. It was like a punch in the gut. I've read where the mental anguish of rejection is in the same region of the brain as physical pain. No wonder it hurts so bad.

Looking back, I realize that most of my pain was self-inflicted. I really took Lisa's leaving hard. I had to take a long look at myself whether I wanted to or not. In fact, I saw three different Christian counselors. All of them came to the same conclusion. I wasn't just feeling rejected, I was feeling abandoned. Not only from my wife, but my father dying several years before, my mother dying, my aunt, my cousin, my dog. I was forced to digest a stew of awful emotions.

I tried to focus on God and Evan though. I knew I needed to be thankful for what I did have in my life instead of looking at what I didn't have. It took me months to see what God had blessed me with, not what the devil was trying to take away.

I had tried over and over to reconcile with Lisa but I wasn't successful. You see, divorce was not what I wanted. Never in a million years. I can say with all honesty that there was no infidelity on my part, nor did I ever physically abuse her. All I wanted was for our family to be together. I tried everything I could think of to keep us from breaking up. In the end, none of it was enough. Nothing that I said or did made a difference.

Not only did I feel rejection and abandonment, but fear. I realized what divorce meant, that my covenant with God would be broken. I made vows to stay married until the day I died. I knew the impact that it would have on me and Evan. It was all terrifying.

The ton of emotions at times were too much. I would sit and cry over my inability to keep our family whole. All I could do was go to God and ask for forgiveness and strength.

There were two big positives from the separation and divorce though, I drew closer to God and Evan than ever before. I spent time with both of them and it was healing to my soul. I dove into the words of The Bible and found peace and comfort I so desperately needed. I read about the extreme struggles that Jesus had with rejection and abandonment and that encouraged me more than anything.

Jesus faced rejection in Luke 9:51-56 NIV. I also saw how Jesus responded to it. *"As the time approached for him to be taken up to heaven, Jesus resolutely set out for Jerusalem. And he sent messengers on ahead, who went into a Samaritan village to get things ready for him; but the people there did not welcome him, because he was heading for Jerusalem. When the disciples James and John saw this, they asked, 'Lord, do you want us to call fire down from heaven to destroy them?' But Jesus turned and rebuked them. Then he and his disciples went to another village."* Jesus didn't turn around or give up. He continued on His mission.

Jesus felt the sting of those two dreadful emotions many times in The Bible. His family members (John 7:5), His friends (John 13:21), His community (Matthew 13:57), and even His own Father (Matthew 27:46).

He rose above it...literally! He persevered. I used His story to guide me and I was able to find my way through the darkness. God doesn't want us confused, anxious, depressed or feeling unwanted. No way. We are His children.

"And will be a Father unto you, and ye shall be my sons and daughters, saith the Lord Almighty." -2 Corinthians 6:18 KJV

"I praise you because I am fearfully and wonderfully made; your works are wonderful, I know that full well." -Psalm 139:14 NIV

"Give thanks to the God of heaven. His love for us endures forever." -Psalm 136:26 NIV

"So don't be afraid; you are more valuable than a whole flock of sparrows." -Matthew 10:31 NLT

"I will not leave you as orphans; I will come to you." -John 14:18 NIV

Thankfully I realized that early on in the separation that the devil was behind all the doubt and unrest. Once I unveiled the true culprit behind all the turmoil, I was able to deal with it a lot better. He comes to steal, kill and destroy. To steal my joy, to kill my self-esteem and to destroy my marriage. He'll stop at nothing to make life on this earth as difficult as he can for us all.

My Christian upbringing, prayers from friends and family, my devotion to God and my awareness of Satan kept me from spinning out of control. I knew God would be there for me. He would see me through. Praise His Holy Name!

"One who has unreliable friends soon comes to ruin, but there is a friend who sticks closer than a brother." -Proverbs 18:24 NIV

CHAPTER SEVENTEEN:
DIAMOND GIRL

"For his anger endureth but a moment; in his favour is life: weeping may endure for a night, but joy cometh in the morning."
-Psalm 30:5 KJV

It was only after I heard that Lisa was seeing someone else that I started the process of dating, even though I didn't want to. It was hard at first because every time I'd look at a girl in that way, I felt I was cheating. I didn't want to get into a relationship feeling that way. It wouldn't be fair to the girl.

As the days and nights went by, the heartbreak started to dissipate and so did the guilt. I could feel God nudging me forward. I wanted to move on respectfully. I didn't want to make a spectacle of the divorce online. I never wanted to slam Lisa and say it was all her fault when I knew deep down that I was partly responsible for her unhappiness. All I can say is that I tried to do the right thing.

My friends and family encouraged me to start making steps to go on with my life. My primary focus was Evan. During the separation, I went on a vacation with him to Florida, just me and him. I wanted to let him know he was loved and everything was going to be alright.

I also didn't want him to think that Dad would move on to another woman too fast. I wanted him to know that I respected his mother and that I gave it my all. He needed to see that in me. If I moved too quickly, he might have thought that I didn't love his mom like I said I did. So, I inched forward until I was finally able to start the search for a new life.

Eventually I went out on a few coffee dates and really enjoyed the conversation. It was more like getting together with friends though. The conversations would somehow always lead back to the divorce and my struggle with it. It was awkward to say the least. I had no clue as to how to be a single guy at my age. All the other single men I knew used online dating apps to try and find someone, but I just couldn't seem to muster up the interest to do that.

I did however meet a couple of women on Facebook. At least I knew they were real on that website. I had some really good conversations and could finally see myself coming out of my shell. One girl lived in Florida. She told me on the phone that she had already planned a trip to Nashville prior to us talking. So, when she came to town, we were able to hang out for a day or two.

We had a wonderful time together but we were just on two separate pages. She was a beautiful lady. She was a nurse and had two kids from a previous marriage. We had a lot in common, but just not enough. She lived in another state and it was just too far away for us to have a serious relationship. I wasn't about to try and make her move to Tennessee when we didn't know it was going to work out between us or not. That wouldn't have been fair for her or her children. It was also just too early for me to commit.

There was another girl that caught my attention for a while but the same thing happened, there were just too many differences between us. During that time, I never made a "I'm available now" post on Facebook. I didn't really know how to let everyone know what was going on in my life. Somehow or the other people started to realize that I was going through a divorce. Maybe it was because Lisa had started posting pictures of her and the new man she was with on her page.

While my love life was trying to bloom my financial life had taken a big blow to the bow. If I didn't do something quick, I was going down. When the divorce was finalized Lisa and I split everything equally. I had to refinance the house because Evan wanted to keep it. I wanted to give him some stability in the chaos. To refinance it, I knew it was going to be a strain on me. Even if I did keep it, I couldn't keep it long unless I started working hard again.

I started playing shows. Any gig that would come up I would do. Gordon and I played all kinds of songwriter shows together. I played the famous Bluebird Cafe four or five times that year with him, Danny Flowers and Karla Davis.

One day Gordon said he wanted to introduce me to a non-profit organization that he had been involved with in the past. He thought it'd be good for me and my mental health. It was a way to give back to the community, and donate some of my time. It was an organization called The Heimerdinger Foundation.

I went over one day to their headquarters in Green Hills and saw for myself the wonderful deeds they do. Calvary United Methodist Church let them use their kitchen and grounds to further their cause. The foundation is made up of volunteers that prepare and deliver organic meals to cancer patients in the Nashville area. They even had their own garden where they can pick their own vegetables for their meals.

I met with Kathie Heimerdinger, the founder and Katharine Ray the executive director. They were some of the nicest ladies I've ever met in my life. Gordon and I let them know that we'd like to donate our time and talent to help them raise money and awareness for their mission. They were so overwhelmed that they cried. God was at work.

I let them know that Mom had cancer before she passed and if I had known about their services when she was sick, it would've been so appreciated. Taking care of someone with cancer is a full-time job, and what they were literally bringing to the table, was priceless.

For the next year or so Gordon and I helped raise over $20,000 for their cause. I look back now and know that God used my divorce to get me involved with them. He knew that it would soothe my soul and help sick people at the same time. I urge whomever is reading this to give, if you can, to their foundation. https://www. heimerdingerfoundation.com/donate/. May it soothe your soul like it did mine.

Life changed dramatically for me. I felt more connected to God's purpose and felt like I had become a better father to Evan. We'd spend the day walking or riding bicycles together. I was more involved in his school work and spent more time at night putting him to bed. I had learned not to take my time with him for granted.

I was brainstorming constantly about how to generate some commerce. I considered trying to find a publishing deal, maybe make a new record, maybe start a band, possibly even get into the record business. I had options, but I knew they would take time. The first thing I felt like doing was to finish this book. I knew that even if no one bought it at least Evan would have my story in print. That was enough for me to start in on it.

The other was to start making a record that included some of the hits from my family. Since I'm cousins with Dan Seals (England Dan and John Ford Coley) and Jimmy Seals (Seals & Crofts), Chuck Seals and Troy Seals why wouldn't I make a cool record of all their songs.

It was time to appreciate my past, look forward to the future and make the most of every single day I have on this planet. It was the time to reflect and do what God was telling me to do. I prayed for His guidance and for His Will to be done in my life.

I remember having a meeting with my friend Brian Eckert and we were talking about the possibility of finding new talented artists to work with and possibly write and produce some projects together. I told him I loved the idea, but I just didn't see myself going out at night to noisy clubs to find them. That evening I went on Facebook and somehow or the other I saw her profile.

She was young and beautiful, and when I clicked on her I noticed a picture of her with headphones on and singing. I thought to myself if she can sing as good as she looks, I could work with her. I messaged her and said, "Hey Deni. I'm not sure where I saw your profile but you seem like a sweet girl. I see that you love The Lord. We have that in common:-) Are you a singer songwriter?" I went on to say, "I'm probably old enough to be your dad so I'm not hitting on you:-) Just curious what your voice sounds like."

She responded by saying, "Yes I sing." She then let me know I could search her videos and hear her sing. A few days later I listened and was very impressed but at that point I had already started thinking that I should concentrate on starting my Seals family album instead of producing someone else. I didn't want to waste her time and promise her things I couldn't deliver.

Several weeks later I logged on to Facebook and noticed that she liked a few of my photos. I'd find out later that my profile picture was the main reason why she paid any attention to me at all. Somehow, I found a picture on the internet of a man that was dressed up to look like Jesus, with the classic white robe and long flowing hair walking down a rocky coastal beach with the waves crashing against them. The Jesus character was consoling and guiding the man through the stormy weather. From behind, the man Jesus had his arm around looked eerily like me. It compelled Deni to look deeper into who I was.

When I saw that she had been rummaging through my photos, I thought there was no way a young pretty girl like her would be interested in an old dude like me. To be courteous, I went on her page and liked a few of her pictures just so she'd know I thought she was beautiful. I didn't think any more about it.

A day or two later I was pleasantly surprised when she messaged me saying she liked a video that I posted and she thought it was funny. Nervously, I messaged back and asked if I could call her sometime and she said yes. When I called, she had a soft country accent that was soothing and very attractive. She told me she was twenty-three and I told her I was forty-eight. We were twenty-five years apart!

At first it was absurd for me to think we would date at all. I could be friendly and maybe hang out a few times, but that was about it. I thought that we would probably be on two separate pages when it came to life. I had no expectations whatsoever.

After a few conversations I realized that she was a really sweet girl from a small town just south of Franklin called Chapel Hill, Tennessee. She had been born in Nashville, but she moved out to the country when she was a child. I also realized that even though she loved singing, she didn't want to be a professional singer. She was really shy and didn't like the lifestyle of having to be out on the road all the time meeting and greeting people.

We talked for a month before we ever saw one another. Our talks would sometimes last five or six hours. She told me all about her past love life and I shared mine. We both were Christians and felt the same way about politics. Actually, there wasn't much we didn't see eye to eye on. It surprised us both. She was an old soul and I had a young heart. Somehow, we seemed to relate in the middle.

The first night we met I drove down to her house in the country to pick her up. Neither of us were too excited about going out somewhere, so we just came back to my house to hang out and watch a movie. When I pulled up to her house and got a glimpse of her for the first time I thought to myself, "Oh no...she's gorgeous...now what?"

We drove off into the night and started seeing one another every chance we could. We'd go driving at night and just talk. We'd listen to music together and I'd share road stories. She'd tell me about her upbringing and I'd tell her about mine.

I asked her one day, "Do you think your dad will approve of us seeing each other because of our age difference?" She said she thought he wouldn't mind at all. And sure enough, several months later she told him about us seeing one another and he was good with it. He just wanted to make sure I treated her right. That was a big deal for me. I certainly didn't want to continue to see her, if her father wasn't cool with it.

Deni had the same kind of crazy humor as I did and we kept each other in stitches all the time. We would laugh...I mean really laugh. It brought me the joy that I really needed in my life. I could tell that the laughter was medicine for her as well. We had both had our heart's broken badly, and now we had each other to lean on and trust in.

Deni Baker and Brady Seals

One day she told me she'd been dealing with nerve issues in her legs where they would shake sometimes uncontrollably and she also said she'd get dizzy out of the blue. It worried me. That didn't seem right. I told her that she needed to see a doctor and get to the bottom of it.

She agreed and we scheduled a time to go see a neurologist. She wasn't able to actually see the doctor, but she saw her nurse instead. Deni told the nurse what had been going on with her and the nurse told her that it might be MS (Multiple Sclerosis) and she needed to make another appointment. She issued an MRI to scan her brain to see if that was the case.

Deni and I were both very concerned and started to find out more about the potentially debilitating disease. In the process of it all, she was also complaining that her heart was racing a lot and was concerned about that too. Again, we scheduled to see a heart doctor.

For several months we had to wait for her to see both doctors. She worried a lot and just like me, she had anxiety. Both of us suffered from that. We'd pray together and I would try to comfort her and let her know that everything will work out for God's glory.

Finally, we were able to see both doctors. The neurologist looked at the MRI and told us that she was certain that it wasn't MS. She didn't see any lesions on her brain and she felt the shaking and dizziness was from anxiety. The cardiologist gave her a clean bill of health as well. He said the same thing...anxiety.

We both celebrated the fact that she didn't have something more severe. We thanked the Lord, and Deni felt like she had a brighter future ahead. Through it all I was getting more attached to her. It scared me though. I didn't know if I was quite ready for a serious relationship. In fact, we broke up two or three times because we were both concerned that we weren't prepared to jump into the deep end of love.

Somehow or the other we got through it all though. Eight months into us seeing one another I told her I loved her. She had told me she loved me a month before. I cared a lot for her then and thought I might be falling in love too but I wanted to wait and make sure. I also told her not to break my heart. I didn't want to go through that again.

We went on several trips together and had a ball. The one that sticks out the most was Gatlinburg. I had been asked to be a part of the Smoky Mountains Songwriter Festival and she went with me. We stayed for about five days. We walked around town hand in hand and just loving life. God had brought me a long way in a short time. He had brought me love.

All the while Deni and I were seeing each other I had a few musical projects going on. While working on the Seals family album I called Lua Crofts, Dash Crofts' daughter. I asked her if she would come over sometime and sing background on a few of her dad's songs that I was recording.

Lua and I hadn't seen each other since the '90s. When she came over, we started singing "Diamond Girl" by Seals & Crofts. It was magical. Our voices blended immediately. We both were taken aback by it. We sang another one too, "Get Closer," and that was even better! I knew we were onto something. I said, "Lua if you want, let's learn a few songs and get together again soon and see if there might be something here." She agreed completely and we scheduled a time to sing again.

The second time we were a little more rehearsed and we were spot on. It was obvious that we needed to try and do a duo thing and figure out what we needed to do next. I called Gordon and we set a date to record, "Summer Breeze" over at his place along with his friends, Blair Masters and Andy Hubbard.

The session was awesome. Lua came over and sang her parts and it sounded like a record. Gordon added all of the guitar and bass parts, Andy recorded his percussion stuff and Blair laid down the keyboard tracks. It was all very organic and acoustic sounding. We all knew there was something special about it.

Lua and I decided to call it *Seals & Crofts 2*. Dash was actually the one that suggested the roman numeral two but, in the end, we settled on the number 2 just to make it easy for people to remember. I built a website and we put together an EPK (electronic press kit) so people could see and hear what we were all about.

Seals & Crofts 2
Brady Seals and Lua Crofts Faragher
Photo Credit: Lindsey Freitas

It didn't take long to get a few dates on the calendar. We'd go out as a four-piece band. Me, Lua, Gordon and Andy. It was such an honor to be out playing some of the Seals & Crofts hits. With Lua being Dash's daughter and me being a cousin of Jimmy, it was obvious we had to give it a go. Jimmy and Dash loved what we were doing and gave us their full blessing to continue.

The other project that I got involved with was The Petty Junkies. My old friend Lonnie Wilson called me up one day and asked if I'd be interested in being in a Tom Petty tribute band. At first, he just wanted me to sing background harmonies and play guitar. He explained that they planned on playing a lot locally and it wouldn't get in the way of any other gig I may have.

I loved the thought of it. When he told me who was in the band I jumped at the opportunity. Mark Hill was going to be the band leader. He was the bass player and sang background harmonies. Lonnie was on drums and singing backgrounds. Gordon Kennedy had said yes to playing guitar and singing. Pat Buchanan was going to front the band and sing the lead vocals.

I said, "Heck yes, count me in!" All of those guys had been some of the top studio musicians in town for years and years. These guys were the best of the best.

Lonnie called me back within a week or so and said Pat had dropped out. I told him, "Dude...I can sing me some Tom Petty." I wanted to throw my name in the hat to front the band. I had been a huge Petty fan all my life and knew most of the songs anyways. They agreed to give me a chance and we scheduled a rehearsal over at Lonnie's music room.

I made sure I had my stuff together by the time rehearsal rolled around. I tried to capture the inflections of Tom's vocal but still not lose my character in it. I even learned the harmonica part that was on "Mary Jane's Last Dance". It only took one song in rehearsal and the boys told me I had the job.

Everyone showed up prepared and it sounded incredible. I couldn't believe just how much it sounded like Tom's records. Jerry McPherson had been asked to be the second guitar player and he was stellar! The dude can play!

The band got along great too. There was laughter and stories after every song we played. It seemed like we were meant to be. All of us were veterans in the business and we knew what kind of dedication we'd need to learn a 90-minute Petty set. We didn't want to botch it up. We wanted people to walk away from hearing us thinking that we did Tom Petty justice.

The Petty Junkies
From left to right: Gordon Kennedy, Blair Masters, Brady Seals, Lonnie Wilson, Mark Hill and Jerry McPherson

We all had reputations to uphold. Everybody had been very successful in their own right. Well over 300 hit songs had been penned, played on, sung, or produced by the members of the band. Three of the players had also written multiple hit songs throughout the years. I was as proud as I could be to be a part of it.

It took us six months to prepare for our first gig. It was hard to get us all together at the same time because everyone was so busy. We played a little place in Columbia, TN to work out our first show jitters. We killed it.

Deni didn't know what to think of my profession. Everyday life for an artist is very inconsistent. One day you're extremely busy and the next you're sitting around staring at the walls. She's very reserved, so going to shows and being around a lot of people was a shock to her system. I think overall, she liked it though.

For months Deni and I discussed when it would be appropriate for her to meet Evan. I wanted to make sure he'd be comfortable doing that. I didn't want to throw too much at him too fast. After ten months of Deni and I seeing each other, I felt it was time.

Nashville Sounds Baseball Game
From left to right: Deni Baker, Brady Seals and Evan Seals

They liked each other right off the bat. Deni was so sweet to him and he seemed to really enjoy her company.

We all hung out and it couldn't have gone better. It felt so good to have a female in the house and for all of us to do things together. Again, God had somehow got Evan and me through some trying times and gifted us with joy once again.

HEALING HAPPENS

Sometimes it's instant, sometimes it takes a while and sometimes it doesn't happen at all. The Gospels are filled with stories of Jesus healing all kinds of bodily affliction. God still works miracles to this day in ways that defy medical knowledge. His Word says for us to pray for what we need. The rest is up to Him. His Will is sufficient. *"And he said unto me, My grace is sufficient for thee: for my strength is made perfect in weakness. Most gladly therefore will I rather glory in my infirmities, that the power of Christ may rest upon me." -2 Corinthians 12:9 KJV*

I don't know why God doesn't heal every affliction. But the Bible does promise that if we are not healed in this life, there is something greater awaiting us in heaven.

Some preachers say if we have enough faith we can be healed on command. Some say we have to eliminate the sin in our lives. Some even claim that there are certain techniques in how we pray that will unleash God's curing powers. The Bible even says that the Holy Spirit that dwells within us will pray for us when we can't. *"Likewise the Spirit also helpeth our infirmities: for we know not what we should pray for as we ought: but the Spirit itself maketh intercession for us with groanings which cannot be uttered." -Romans 8:26 KJV*

I don't know exactly how to make God do what I want Him to do, but I do know that I serve a God that is capable of doing the impossible.

"But Jesus beheld them, and said unto them, With men this is impossible; but with God all things are possible." -Matthew 19:26 KJV

"For with God nothing shall be impossible." -Luke 1:37 KJV

I trusted in God in my weakest hours. When I was at my lowest, I could still feel God's presence. He never left me. I never gave up hope. Darkness did not completely consume me. There was always His little light shining to let me know He was there. God continues to renew my mind and heal my broken heart. Thank You Jesus!

"Bless the Lord, O my soul,
And forget not all his benefits:
Who forgiveth all thine iniquities;
Who healeth all thy diseases;
Who redeemeth thy life from
destruction; Who crowneth thee with
lovingkindness and tender mercies;
Who satisfieth thy mouth with good
things; So that thy youth is renewed
like the eagle's." -Psalm 103:2-5 KJV

CHAPTER EIGHTEEN:
ROOTS RUN DEEP

"Blessed be the God and Father of our Lord Jesus Christ,
who hath blessed us with all spiritual blessings in heavenly places
in Christ:" -Ephesians 1:3 KJV

I've been on this spinning rock for fifty-one years now, and each sunrise brings a new surprise. But God has been the one constant thing in my life. It says in Hebrews 13:8 KJV that *"Jesus Christ the same yesterday, and to day, and for ever."* He is the one I'm able to rely on when times get rough, and the one I can praise when blessings come my way. I'm so grateful to my mother for her devotion to God and bringing me to church. I'm also thankful to my grandmother and my great-grandmother. Christianity has been a way of life for me.

As a child, I dreamed of being a firefighter, to be a hero. I wanted to be a soldier, to be a patriot. I chose to be a Christian so I could go to heaven and help save someone from the torment of hell. I know I've strayed at times and made some wrong decisions but I can honestly say that I had the right intentions.

I'm now in a place of peace. Yeah, I still have aches and pains, migraines, stomach issues, and I'm still financially strained, but I'm grateful. I continue to pray each and every day and I think that God is watching out for me and guiding me in the right direction.

Nashville is the place I've called home since I was eighteen. It's changed so much since then that it's almost unrecognizable. Condos have taken the place of recording studios on Music Row. Historic venues and places that meant so much to aspiring artists like myself have been torn down. It's been sad to see that happen in my lifetime. But hopefully the city will remember its musical roots. Maybe there will be new places to keep the music alive in Music City.

Songwriters are an endangered species in 2020. Online piracy has driven most of the writers out of town. There's no way for them to make an honest living anymore. Everyone wants their music free these days. Someone needs to educate and send out a warning signal to inform everyone that the art is dying.

Cell phones and video games are what's popular now, not sitting around a record player and listening to music. Full length CDs aren't desired anymore. Releasing singles and homemade YouTube videos are the norm. I'd give anything for the younger generations to understand the joy and excitement that I had when I was a kid learning and appreciating great music.

I'm still writing and recording and I will continue to do that. Like I said in the preface, I'm planning to release some music that will go hand in hand with this memoir. I also plan on doing a tour next year called "Roots Run Deep". I've hooked up with a booking agency called Live Arts that believes in me and is at this very moment booking performance dates for me. The show is going to be about family...about my roots.

I'm going to be performing some of the hits that God has so graciously blessed me with along with the hits my cousins Seals & Crofts, Dan Seals, Chuck Seals made famous. Songs like "Summer Breeze," "I'd Really Love To See You Tonight" and "Crazy Arms." I'll also be singing songs that my cousin TJ Seals and I wrote for my solo CDs and Hot Apple Pie's records like "Hillbillies." Of course, I won't leave out the classics that uncle Troy wrote like, "Rock & Roll Heart" and "Seven Spanish Angels".

And who knows whether Little Texas or Hot Apple Pie will ever play another show together with the original lineups. I really haven't got a clue. I do know that I've tried my best to mend all the broken fences between me and the guys that I had disagreements with. Four of the guys from the original lineup of Little Texas are still out on the road playing shows without Tim and me. I appreciate each and every one of them for keeping the name alive. Rock on!

Christy DiNapoli and I have worked out any bad blood we ever had between us. He's become a dear friend again and was kind enough to contribute to this book. He is still an advocate of "God Blessed Texas". Not long ago he negotiated another licensing deal with Ford Trucks so they could use the song for their regional "Ford Is The Best In Texas" commercials.

When I co-wrote the song "God Blessed Texas" with Porter Howell back in the '90s, I had no idea that it would make such an impact. I believe that God not only blessed the lyrics and melody of that song, but he did in fact bless Texas and he blessed me too. He's a Mighty God.

It's now the summer of 2020 and as of September 9th, The World Health Organization declared the novel coronavirus (COVID-19) outbreak a global pandemic. The virus started in China and has now spread all over the world at an alarming rate, infecting millions of people. So far there have been over 27.6 million confirmed cases and approximately 898,000 deaths.

Countries such as Italy, Spain and Germany have been hit hard by the disease and the United States tops the list with the most number of cases. Top leaders around the world have issued lockdowns and advised people to stay at home. Businesses have shut down and several months ago, the economy saw its biggest drop since the 2008 recession. The Dow and the FTSE recently saw their biggest one-day declines since 1987.

Fear has set in everywhere. Hand sanitizer, toilet paper, face masks, disinfectant spray and paper towels are on the most wanted list. Several months ago, you couldn't hardly find them anywhere. Once the population realized the severity of the pandemic, everyone rushed to stores to buy up all the supplies.

President Donald Trump and his administration claims that life will go back to normal and there is talk about a vaccine on the horizon. Until then, everyone is advised to bunker down and not to go outside much. Only for essentials. The term "social distancing" is heard all over the news and the phrase "wash your hands constantly and for at least twenty seconds" is all over social media.

Chapter Eighteen: Roots Run Deep

During the stock market drop, I lost nearly $30,000 in two days. I immediately called my stockbroker and told him to pull what money I had left in my retirement funds and put it somewhere safe. Thankfully I was able to move it before the economy sunk even further in the following days.

To add to the chaos, Deni, Evan and I had to move. I had to sell the house that I had been living in for the last twenty years because the financial burden had become too much to bear after the divorce. The idea was to sell the house, buy a lot and build a new home.

Deni and I searched for months and found a beautiful wooded two and half acre lot that seemed perfect for a dream home. I made an offer and the seller accepted it. I had been meeting with a home builder and an architect to construct our new modern rustic home, but the plans were halted just weeks after I purchased the land. I found out my ex-wife was moving to Spring Hill, Tennessee which was a forty-minute drive from the property. I didn't want to be that far from Evan and have to drive every day to and from school.

So with the new information, it forced me to find a place in Spring Hill too. Luckily, we found a new neighborhood home that was perfect for us all. It has a community pool and basketball court. Evan was let down when we said we were going to have to move into a different home than planned. But when he found out the new house had a secret room attached to his bedroom, he lit up and was fine with it.

The last four months have been so stressful. Earlier this year I had to go to the emergency room because my blood pressure was so high. With the pandemic, losing money in the stock market, moving from one house to another, homeschooling Evan and all of my gigs being cancelled, it just about got the best of me.

However, several months ago a ray of light broke through the clouds. I received a much-needed songwriting royalty check in the mail. It couldn't have come at a better time. The Ford commercial that Christy DiNapoli had been working on came to fruition. When I opened up the envelope and saw how much I got paid, I dropped to my knees and thanked God. I'm not gonna lie, I teared up. God blessed me when my family and I needed it most.

I've got a lot to be thankful for today. I pray for those less fortunate. Those who are in bed suffering and sick. For those who have gone bankrupt due to the pandemic. Those who are in harm's way daily, battling this disease. Life for everyone on this planet right now is hard.

I don't know when the stock market will rebound or when the shows will be rebooked, but I know I'll be alright. God is looking out for Evan, Deni and me. From this day forward, I'm going to keep raising my son the best way I can, and continue to let him know that his Dad loves him. I will keep praying for him and showing him the way to heaven. I'm also going to try to get along better with his Mom. Evan needs to know that I appreciate Lisa tremendously for giving him to me.

I'm also going to love Deni, my very own Diamond Girl. Who knows what the future holds for us? Maybe a diamond on her finger? I'm going to let God lead us where He wants us to be. I'm going to learn from any past mistakes and apply my newfound knowledge to our relationship. I'm going to cherish her. To appreciate her and be there for her.

And to wrap things up, if you've taken the time to read this memoir; I thank you from the depths of my heart. I kindly ask for you to take a moment and jot down a good review on Amazon or any other platform you might have downloaded it on. The review truly does help spread the word for the memoir.

I hope that in some way you see through the words of this book what God has done in my life and hopefully you'll see what He's doing in yours. Stay close to Him, trust in Him and spread the wonderful news about how He sent His only Son to die for our sins so we may have everlasting life. May God bless you like He's blessed me.

God Blessed Texas

I've seen a lot of places
I've been around the world
I've seen some pretty faces
Been with some beautiful girls

After all I've witnessed
One thing still amazes me
Just like a miracle,
You have to see to believe

God blessed Texas
With His own hand
Brought down angels
from the promised land

Gave 'em a place
where they could dance
If you wanna see heaven,
brother, here's your chance
I've been sent to spread the message
God blessed Texas

First, He let the sun shine
Then He made the waters deep
Then He gave us moonlight
For all the world to see

Well everybody knows
That the Lord works
in mysterious ways
He took a rest,
Then on the very next day

God blessed Texas
With His own hand
Brought down angels
from the promised land
Gave 'em a place
where they could dance
If you wanna see heaven,
brother, here's your chance
I've been sent to spread the message
God blessed Texas

Words and Music by Porter Howell
and Brady Seals

ABOUT THE AUTHOR

 Brady Seals is related to Jimmy Seals (Seals & Crofts), Dan Seals (England Dan & John Ford Coley), and country songwriters Troy Seals (Songwriting Hall of Fame Member) and Chuck Seals. He has sold over eleven million albums.

Brady is probably best known for his tenure with the country group Little Texas and front man for the band Hot Apple Pie. Little Texas was voted ACM's Vocal Group of the Year Award and received two GRAMMY nominations. As a songwriter, he has celebrated three consecutive number one hits with What Might Have Been, My Love, and God Blessed Texas, granting him the ASCAP Triple Play Award.

Brady is a proud father and Christian. He spends the majority of his time hiking and hanging out with his son and girlfriend in Spring Hill, Tennessee.

Made in the USA
Columbia, SC
10 September 2023

22670627R00150